DATE DUE

FE 1 02		
NO 23 '02		
FE 3 '03		
FE 24 '03		
SE 18 '03		
DE - 1 '03		
	DISCARD	

People to Know

Helen Keller

Lighting the Way for the Blind and Deaf

Carin T. Ford

Enslow Publishers, Inc.

40 Industrial Road | PO Box 38
Box 398 | Aldershot
Berkeley Heights, NJ 07922 | Hants GU12 6BP
USA | UK

http://www.enslow.com

Library of Congress Cataloging-in-Publication Data

Ford, Carin T.
    Helen Keller : lighting the way for the blind and deaf / Carin T. Ford.
        p. cm. — (People to know)
    Includes bibliographical references and index.
    Summary: Discusses the life and accomplishments of Helen Keller, who was left
blind and deaf by illness at a young age, overcame these handicaps, and spent the
rest of her life working to improve conditions for other handicapped people.
    ISBN 0-7660-1530-0
    1. Keller, Helen, 1880-1968—Juvenile literature. 2. Blind-deaf women—United
States—Biography—Juvenile literature. [1. Keller, Helen, 1880-1968. 2. Blind.
3. Deaf. 4. Physically handicapped. 5. Women—Biography.] I. Title. II. Series.
HV1624.K4 F67   2000
362.4'1'092—dc21   00-008979

Printed in the United States of America

10 9 8 7 6 5 4 3 2 1

To Our Readers:
All Internet Addresses in this book were active and appropriate when we went to press.
Any comments or suggestions can be sent by e-mail to Comments@enslow.com or to
the address on the back cover.

Illustration Credits: Canadian Heritage-Parks Canada, Alexander Graham
Bell National Historic Site, Baddeck, Nova Scotia, p, 62; Courtesy of the
American Foundation for the Blind, Helen Keller Archives, pp. 4, 67, 74;
Courtesy of the National Federation of the Blind, p. 25; Helen Keller Property
Board, Tuscumbia, Alabama, pp. 8, 15, 32; National Archives, pp. 57, 100;
Perkins School for the Blind, pp. 27, 37, 43, 46, 48, 54, 77, 82, 87, 97.

Cover Illustration: Library of Congress

Contents

Helen Keller, age seven.

"No-world"

Helen Keller kicked wildly. Blind, deaf, and unable to talk since infancy, the six-year-old child did not know where she was. She had been taken from her home—away from her mother, father, and baby sister—and brought to a different house.

But, then, everything had been different lately.

The week before, on March 3, 1887, a stranger had come to live with Helen's family. The stranger was a young woman who made Helen wash her hands, comb her hair, and button her boots. No matter how much Helen cried and shrieked, the strange woman made her eat with a spoon instead of grabbing the food with her hands. The stranger also continually moved her fingers against Helen's palm, forming them into different positions. Helen had always been a curious child and the finger movements caught her attention.

"I was at once interested in this finger play and tried to imitate it," she wrote years later.[1]

But now Helen was more than curious. She was angry at being alone with this woman and homesick for her family.[2]

When supper was served that night, Helen ate all her food, although she would not let the woman touch her. Helen played with her dolls until bedtime and then put on her nightclothes. But she refused to go to bed. She kicked and clawed at the woman for close to two hours. The woman's strength and persistence eventually wore Helen down, and she curled up near the edge of the bed and went to sleep.[3]

Helen's feelings of anger and homesickness did not disappear overnight. When the woman gave Helen clothes to put on the next morning, Helen threw them down on the floor and would not wear them.

She preferred to spend much of her time standing at the front door, her hand to her cheek. This was a sign Helen used to show she wanted her mother. After touching her cheek, she would sorrowfully shake her head. Helen's mother was not coming; Helen had been left alone with a strange woman in a strange house.

As the days passed, the woman slowly began to see a change in Helen. She did not fly into a rage every time the woman corrected her behavior or asked Helen to do something. The wild child was becoming gentler and would even occasionally sit in the woman's lap.[4]

Helen also continued learning new finger positions. But to Helen, these gestures were no different from other signs she had invented to communicate with her family from her dark, silent world.

"A shake of the head meant 'No' and a nod, 'Yes,' a pull meant 'Come' and a push, 'Go,'" she later wrote. "Was it bread that I wanted? Then I would imitate the acts of cutting the slices and buttering them. If I wanted my mother to make ice-cream for dinner I made the sign for working the freezer and shivered, indicating the cold."[5]

Within a few weeks, the two had moved back in with Helen's family, and Helen had learned the finger positions for the following words: doll, pin, key, dog, hat, cup, box, water, candy, eye, fingers, toe, head, cake, baby, mother, sit, stand, walk, knife, fork, spoon, saucer, tea, papa, bed, run, mug, and milk.

These last two words gave her the most trouble. In Helen's mind, the finger movements for *mug* and *milk* meant the same thing—something to drink. No matter which word she used, Helen would accompany the finger motions with an imitation of drinking.

The woman thought of a way to straighten out the problem. She took Helen outside to the water pump and had her hold her mug under the spout. Lifting and lowering the handle, the woman pumped cold water into the mug until the water was flowing over Helen's hand. Into Helen's other hand the woman spelled *w-a-t-e-r*, moving her fingers slowly at first and then more quickly.

The date was April 5, 1887. It was a date Helen would never forget.

"I stood still, my whole attention fixed upon the motions of her fingers," Helen wrote. "Suddenly I felt a misty consciousness as of something forgotten—a thrill of returning thought; and somehow the mystery of language was revealed to me. I knew then that 'w-a-t-e-r' meant the wonderful cool something that was flowing over my hand. That living word awakened my soul, gave it light, hope, joy, set it free!"[6]

Now Helen understood the connection between the finger movements and the objects they represented. Her face lit up as she spelled "water" into the woman's hand, over and over. Helen then fell to the ground and

W-a-t-e-r. *At this water pump, Helen, blind and deaf, grasped the key to language—that every object and every action has a name.*

asked the woman to spell *its* name. She wanted to know the name of everything! Eagerly, she pointed to the pump and the trellis, waiting for the woman to spell the words into her hand.

Suddenly, she turned to the woman.

What was *her* name?

The woman reached for Helen's hand and spelled, "T-e-a-c-h-e-r."

Anne Sullivan was Teacher. She had arrived a month earlier and broken through the silent darkness of what Helen later described as her "no-world."[7]

As Helen excitedly left the water pump and headed back to the house, she was determined to know the name of every object and every action. She learned thirty new words within only a few hours, including *mother, father, sister, door, open, shut, give, go,* and *come.*

But the work was just beginning.

From Light to Dark

There were many disagreements over the years between Captain Arthur Henley Keller and his wife, Kate Adams. One of them concerned what to name their first daughter.

Captain Keller wanted to name her Mildred Campbell, after one of his relatives. But Kate Keller favored the name Helen Everett, for her mother. As Captain Keller carried his infant daughter to church for the christening, he remembered only that the child was to be named for her grandmother. She was christened Helen Adams Keller.

Helen was born on June 27, 1880, in Tuscumbia, Alabama, in a two-room cottage located forty feet from Ivy Green, the family's main house. The little cottage was covered with yellow roses and honeysuckle, and

Helen lived there with a nurse for the first year and a half of her life.

The name Helen means "light," and it seemed appropriate for the blue-eyed, curly-haired child who was both outgoing and extremely intelligent. At only six months old, Helen was able to say "How d'ye" for "How do you do." She also said "tea, tea, tea" and "wah-wah," which she knew meant water. By the time Helen was one year old, she was taking her first steps.

Although Helen grew up on a 640-acre estate, her family was not wealthy. Her father owned a cotton plantation and was also the editor of a weekly news-paper, the *North Alabamian*. In 1885, he was appointed U.S. marshal of the northern district of Alabama by President Grover Cleveland.

Kate Keller worked from morning until night try-ing to keep expenses down. She sewed, cooked, grew her own fruits and vegetables, raised livestock, and made her own butter, bacon, ham, pickles, and jellies.

It was a hard life for Kate Keller, who had been pampered as a child and had never had to worry about money. Her father was a lawyer who served as a brigadier general in the Confederate Army during the Civil War. But the family had its roots in New England, with ties to William Tecumseh Sherman, a leading Union general during the Civil War. Kate was also related to Edward Everett, a clergyman who had spoken on the same platform with President Abraham Lincoln at Gettysburg. When the war ended, Kate's family had moved from Arkansas to Tennessee, where she lived a life of luxury.

That existence ended in 1878 when Kate turned

twenty-two and married Captain Keller. The two had vastly different backgrounds, personalities, and interests, and by the time Helen was born, Kate knew she had made a mistake in marrying the captain.[1]

A staunch southerner, Captain Keller had fought in the Civil War and was related to Robert E. Lee, commander in chief of the Confederate armies. While Kate Keller enjoyed reading in her spare time, Captain Keller was fond of fishing and hunting.

His first wife had died in 1877, at age thirty-eight, and the forty-two-year-old Captain Keller married Kate a year later. He had two sons from his first marriage— James, in his twenties, and William Simpson, thirteen. Although the younger boy got along with his new stepmother, James resented Kate Keller for filling his mother's place only a year after her death.

Kate Keller disliked admitting there were problems in her life; she was an aloof, private person. Yet sometimes she would go for days without speaking to her husband, and the lines of tension about her mouth showed "all that she had suffered," according to a friend of Helen's.[2]

Family troubles were put aside when Helen was nineteen months old. "Then came the illness which closed my eyes and ears and plunged me into the unconsciousness of a newborn baby," she recalled.[3]

Helen later said she remembered feeling as if someone had lifted her into a bright light. "I felt a great pain which made me scream violently," she said.[4]

The illness that struck Helen in February 1882 came on suddenly. She developed a high fever, and the family doctor did not think the child would survive. The doctor labeled it "acute congestion of the stomach and brain." Modern-day physicians have speculated that the illness might have been either scarlet fever or meningitis, an inflammation of the linings of the brain and spinal cord.

Helen later wrote of her mother's attempts to soothe her during the "hours of fret and pain, and the agony and bewilderment with which I awoke after a tossing half sleep, and turned my eyes, so dry and hot, to the wall, away from the once-loved light, which came to me dim and yet more dim each day."[5]

Helen's parents did not at first realize their daughter had been left blind and deaf as a result of the illness. The fever left as quickly as it had come, and Helen slept heavily.

"When I awoke and found that all was dark and still, I suppose I thought it was night and I must have wondered why day was so long in coming," she said. "Gradually, however, I got used to the silence and darkness that surrounded me and forgot that it had ever been day."[6]

As Kate Keller ran her hand in front of her daughter's face one day, she realized Helen's eyes did not blink or close. There was also no response from Helen when the dinner bell rang.

Feeling desperately sorry for their daughter, Kate and Captain Keller could not bring themselves to discipline her. Helen would run wildly about the house, smashing lamps and dishes, throwing china and silverware, thrusting her hands into the food on people's plates during mealtime, and often causing physical harm to anyone around her. Her grandmother

Adams was forced to flee the room when Helen began pinching her.

"I think I knew when I was naughty," Helen wrote later.[7] Yet she continued to misbehave when she did not get what she wanted.

Captain Keller's sister, Eveline—called "Aunt Ev"— traveled with Helen and her mother to Eureka Springs, Arkansas, and stayed for six weeks in hopes that the "curative waters" there might help the child. But there did not seem to be any way of helping Helen, and eventually her ability to speak vanished along with her eyesight and hearing.

Unable to communicate, Helen became extremely frustrated and frequently threw tantrums. She was aware that only *she* made signs; her family and friends communicated with their mouths. "Sometimes I stood between two people who were conversing and touched their lips," she wrote. "I could not understand and was vexed. I moved my lips and gesticulated frantically without result. This made me so angry at times that I kicked and screamed until I was exhausted."[8]

When Helen was five, her sister, Mildred, was born. Helen became so jealous of Mildred that she once dumped the baby out of the cradle, nearly killing her.

Some relatives advised the Kellers to put Helen in a mental institution. They claimed that Helen's brain had been affected by the illness and she would never learn to behave properly.[9] They regarded Helen as an uncontrollable monster. But Kate Keller would not consider putting her child in an institution. So Helen hung on to her mother's dress much of the day, rubbing

Ivy Green, the Keller family home in Tuscumbia, Alabama. Trapped in her dark, silent world, young Helen often threw wild tantrums, smashing lamps and throwing dishes. The smaller building is the cottage where Helen was born.

her hands against her mother's face so often that the skin fell off Kate Keller in patches.

Aunt Ev steadfastly maintained that Helen had "more sense than all the Kellers, if there is any way to reach her mind."[10] Helen had, in fact, devised sixty signs as a way of communicating. The signs were based on her keen ability to imitate every motion and object she sensed. They included knotting her hair at the back of her head or touching her cheek to indicate her mother; tying the strings of a bonnet under her chin to signify her aunt; and sucking her fingers to indicate her baby sister. She imitated her father by sitting in his armchair with a newspaper and wearing his glasses.

By the age of five, Helen had learned to fold and put away the clean laundry; she could distinguish her own clothing from the rest of her family's. She also learned how to use a key, and one day she locked her mother in the pantry for several hours. While Kate Keller banged on the door to be released from the pantry, Helen sat on the porch steps, laughing.

Although she was locked in a dark, silent world, Helen could understand a good deal of what was happening around her. One day, she became aware through the vibrations of the front door that company was visiting. Helen raced upstairs. Standing in front of a mirror, she put on a dress, poured oil on her hair, and powdered her face. Next, she pinned a veil to her head, and around her waist she tied an overly large bustle—the wire undergarment that made a woman's skirt balloon out in back. With the bustle dangling to the hem of her dress, Helen then went downstairs to help entertain the visitors.

During this time, Helen enjoyed playing with the cook's daughter, Martha Washington. Martha always seemed to understand Helen's signs. Together, the girls worked kneading dough, grinding coffee and spices, making ice cream, and feeding the hens and turkeys.

Under Helen's leadership, the girls often got into trouble. Once they grabbed a cake that had just been frosted and raced away with it. They ate the entire thing, later becoming ill. Another day, they sat cutting out paper dolls. They soon began snipping their shoelaces, the leaves of plants, and then each other's hair.

Helen's actions occasionally had some dangerous consequences, such as the time she dried her wet apron before the sitting-room fire. Annoyed at how long it was taking the apron to dry, she threw it into the fire. Flames leaped up, engulfing Helen and setting her clothes on fire. Her noises caught the attention of a nursemaid, who threw a blanket over Helen and smothered the flames. Still, Helen was left with burns on her hands and charred hair.

Months rolled by and Helen and her family were growing desperate. Helen was tormented by not being able to communicate. "Invisible hands were holding me, and I made frantic efforts to free myself," she said later.[11] Her family longed to find some medical treatment that would allow Helen to see and hear again.

Kate Keller had once read about Laura Bridgman, a young woman who had lost her hearing and sight at the age of two. Laura had been educated at the Perkins Institution for the Blind, in Boston, by Dr. Samuel Gridley Howe, the school's director. Laura was taught to communicate by having the letters of the alphabet traced into her palm.

The English novelist Charles Dickens wrote about meeting Laura in *American Notes*. Kate Keller recalled how Dickens had described Laura's face as "radiant with intelligence and pleasure."[12] She renewed her efforts to find help for Helen.

The Kellers took their daughter to numerous eye doctors throughout Alabama and Tennessee. Everywhere the verdict was the same: Nothing could be done.

Teacher

Kate and Captain Keller refused to give up. They learned of an eye doctor in Baltimore, Maryland, who specialized in hopeless cases. The family made the journey by train, and six-year-old Helen was provided with enough distractions on the trip to keep her fairly calm. She strung shells that had been given to her by one of the passengers, and she followed the conductor as he went about his job. Helen enjoyed using his ticket punch to punch holes of her own in cardboard.

An aunt who was traveling with them put together a doll for Helen out of a towel. Helen quickly perceived that it had no eyes. She pulled two beads off her aunt's cape and tried to indicate what she wanted. The aunt lifted Helen's hand to her own eyes, and Helen nodded. The beads were promptly sewn onto the face of the doll and Helen was content.[1]

Once they arrived in Baltimore, the Kellers met with Dr. Chisholm. After giving Helen a thorough examination, he repeated what all the other doctors had said—Helen's eyesight and hearing would never be restored.

But Dr. Chisholm did offer the Kellers a suggestion. There were schools for the deaf and blind; perhaps Helen could be educated. He recommended that the Kellers see Alexander Graham Bell, a good friend of his, in Washington, D.C. It was a suggestion that would change Helen's life.

Although Bell was famous for inventing the telephone ten years earlier, he was chiefly interested in educating the deaf. Both his mother, Eliza, and his wife, Mabel, were deaf. Bell's father had spent nearly twenty years creating Visible Speech, symbols that were similar to the alphabet but that stood for sounds rather than letters. Long before inventing the telephone, Bell used his father's system to teach speech to deaf children.

At the time the Kellers met Bell, he still devoted most of his energy to working in his laboratory on behalf of people who had speech and hearing problems. Bell and Helen formed an instant friendship that was to last throughout the famous inventor's lifetime. "He held me on his knee while I examined his watch, and he made it strike for me," Helen wrote. "He understood my signs, and I knew it and loved him at once."[2]

Bell advised Captain Keller to contact Michael

Anagnos, the director of the Perkins Institution for the Blind (renamed Perkins School for the Blind in 1955). He told them Anagnos might be able to find a teacher who could work with Helen.

Captain Keller wrote to Anagnos immediately. By January 1887, Anagnos was ready to recommend a teacher—Anne Sullivan.

Sullivan had just graduated from Perkins in 1886 at the head of her class. She was twenty years old and had no idea how she was going to earn a living. She was considering getting a job as a dishwasher or possibly going door-to-door selling books.

In August 1886, Anagnos had written a letter to Sullivan, asking if she "would be disposed to consider favorably an offer of a position in the family of Mr. Keller as governess of his little deaf-mute and blind daughter."[3]

Sullivan had little choice. Alone in the world and with no money, she needed whatever job she could get. Never mind the fact that she had no idea how to go about teaching a spoiled child who was both deaf and blind.[4]

Returning to the Perkins Institution for the Blind to prepare for her new job, Sullivan began studying the history of Laura Bridgman, who was now in her late fifties and still resided at the school. Sullivan read all of Dr. Howe's reports concerning Bridgman's education as well as numerous books on mental development.

Anagnos described Sullivan as "exceedingly intelligent, strictly honest, industrious, ladylike in her manner. . . . Her moral character is all that can be desired."[5] He informed Captain Keller that Sullivan was well acquainted with Bridgman's case and familiar with teaching methods used for children who were unable to see, hear, or speak. Captain Keller agreed to hire Sullivan at $25 a month, including room and board.

Anne Sullivan came from a background that was as full of misfortune as Helen's. Her parents had fled Ireland along with one million other immigrants as a result of the potato famine in the mid-1800s. Born into poverty on April 14, 1866, near Springfield, Massachusetts, Annie—as she was called—developed an eye disease at the age of five. There was no medicine at the time to treat trachoma, and Annie spent much of her youth nearly blind.

She was a rebellious child, difficult to manage. Her father, an alcoholic who worked as a farmhand, often beat his daughter. Annie's mother would help Annie hide from him. In spite of the frequent whippings she received, Annie would often purposely provoke her father until he was furious.[6]

Suffering from the infectious disease tuberculosis, her mother died when Annie turned eight; the family did not even possess enough money to pay for a funeral. Annie's father abandoned his children two years later. Ten-year-old Annie and her five-year-old brother Jimmie, whose hip had been damaged by tuberculosis, were sent to live in the state poorhouse in Tewksbury, Massachusetts, in 1876. A third child, Mary, was healthy and went to live with an aunt. Two other siblings, John and Nellie, had died in infancy.

Annie was almost blind, and Jimmie needed a crutch to walk. The children had no choice but to socialize with the diseased and mentally unstable inmates of the overcrowded poorhouse. The building itself was filthy and overrun with rats and cockroaches. Years later, Sullivan described Tewksbury as both cruel and gruesome.[7]

Three months after arriving at the poorhouse, Jimmie died. Annie was now entirely on her own.

"I believe very few children have ever been so completely left alone as I was," she wrote. "I felt that I was the only thing that was alive in the world. . . . Not a ray of light shone in the great darkness which covered me that day."[8]

Annie had several operations on her eyes during her stay at Tewksbury, but they were not successful. She heard from the inmates that there were schools for the blind, and it became her dream to attend one.

When a committee from the state board of charities visited the poorhouse one day, Annie followed the group of men. She had been told that the committee chairman's name was Frank B. Sanborn. Not only was Sanborn on the board of trustees at the Perkins Institution, he was also close friends with the school's director, Michael Anagnos.

Suddenly, Annie threw herself toward them and, unable to see clearly enough to distinguish one person from another, cried out, "Mr. Sanborn, Mr. Sanborn, I want to go to school!"[9]

They asked what was wrong with her, and Annie replied that she could not see very well. When they asked how long she had been at the poorhouse, Annie was unable to remember.

Some time after this incident, Annie was told she was leaving Tewksbury and going to school. She left the poorhouse at the age of fourteen and would spend the rest of her life trying to forget her childhood.[10]

Annie arrived at the Perkins Institution for the Blind in Boston, Massachusetts, on October 7, 1880. When she was being admitted, she was asked her name and birthday. She knew her name, although she could not spell it. She did not know her birthday and stated that she was born on the Fourth of July. Annie did not own a hat or a coat, undergarments, a comb, or even a toothbrush. Her first night at the school, she slept in a borrowed nightgown. Feeling even lonelier than she had felt at the poorhouse, Annie cried herself to sleep.[11]

She went through her years at Perkins with her typically rebellious attitude, arguing with students and teachers and coming close to expulsion on several occasions.[12] Anagnos, however, was aware of Sullivan's extreme intelligence, and he never forced her to leave the school.

One of the few friends Annie made at Perkins was Laura Bridgman. Using the manual alphabet and spelling into Laura's hand to communicate, Annie spent a good deal of time with Bridgman, relating interesting current events and gossip to the deaf and blind woman.

After six years, Annie graduated from Perkins. Joyful as she was at being class valedictorian—the top student—Annie was even happier about wearing the beautiful white muslin dress and white slippers she had been given.

But once graduation passed, Annie's joy diminished. She needed to earn a living, yet she had not been trained for any particular occupation. Then she received Anagnos's letter asking if she would be interested in teaching Helen Keller.

On a Monday in early March 1887, Anne Sullivan left Boston headed for Tuscumbia, Alabama. She had never traveled before and had no teaching experience. Sullivan was carrying a doll that had been bought for Helen by the students at Perkins. Laura Bridgman, who taught sewing and needlework at the Perkins Institution, had made clothing for the doll. Sullivan's teaching equipment consisted of some beads and cards, a few books in Braille (which blind people read with their fingertips), a Braille slate, and a stylus.[13]

Sullivan had never been out of Massachusetts, and the journey was not an easy one. She was bundled in heavy clothing that was appropriate for northern weather but not for the South. She had to change trains several times and was frightened when she had to spend the night in Washington, D.C., in a hotel, something she had never done before. Her eyes ached from the cinders and coal dust of the train. Her vision had improved after additional operations, but she had gone through surgery again—to correct crossed eyes—only a few days before her trip. Afraid and alone, Sullivan cried during much of the time she traveled. This further inflamed her eyes.

She finally arrived in Tuscumbia at 6:30 in the evening on Wednesday, March 3, 1887. She was hot,

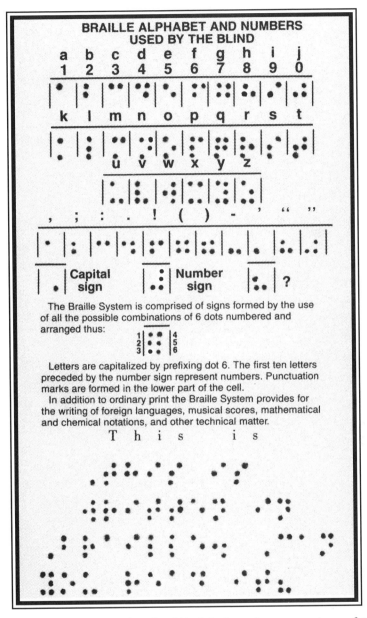

The Braille alphabet for the blind is based on a system of six raised dots that are "read" with the fingertips. (The dots have been colored black so they show in this photograph.) Above is a message in Braille.*

*The message says: This is written in Braille. Can you read it?

frightened, exhausted, and her eyes were red and swollen.

But she did not regret coming. "I felt that the future held something good for me," she wrote.[14]

From the start, Sullivan liked Kate Keller, who had been going to the train station for two days in expectation of the teacher's arrival.

Sullivan was driven to the Kellers' home in a carriage and observed that Tuscumbia reminded her of a New England town, with its blossoming fruit trees and plowed fields. She became "so excited and eager to see my little pupil that I could hardly sit still in my seat. I felt like getting out and pushing the horse along faster."[15]

Helen, meanwhile, was also full of eager anticipation. She stood on the porch, her hair a mess, her pinafore soiled, and her black shoes tied with white laces. Later, she called that day the most important of her life.

"I guessed vaguely from my mother's signs and from the hurrying to and fro in the house that something unusual was about to happen," she wrote. ". . . I felt approaching footsteps. I stretched out my hand, [supposedly] to my mother. Some one took it, and I was caught up. . . ."[16]

Sullivan's impression of Helen was very favorable. She had anticipated a child who was pale and delicate, like Laura Bridgman. But Helen was strong, healthy, and vivacious.

"She has a fine head, and it is set on her shoulders just right," Sullivan wrote. "Her face is hard to describe. It is intelligent, but it lacks mobility, or soul,

"I felt that the future held something good for me," wrote Annie Sullivan, right, after she was hired as Helen's teacher. She did not know then that her success would reach far beyond her dreams.

or something. . . . You can see at a glance that she is blind. One eye is larger than the other and protrudes noticeably. She rarely smiles."[17]

Helen struggled as Sullivan tried to hug her, and she refused to allow her teacher to kiss her. Helen ran her fingers curiously over Sullivan's face, dress, and bag and tried to open the bag, indicating that she thought there would be something good to eat in it. Kate Keller would not let Helen open it and took the bag away. Helen immediately grew red in the face and threw a tantrum, kicking wildly. Sullivan took Helen's hand and put it on her watch. She showed Helen how to open it and it caught the child's interest. The tantrum ended.

Sullivan went up to her room to unpack and Helen trailed after her. Helen helped remove Sullivan's hat and put it on her own head, imitating the gestures of her aunt Ev by tilting her head from side to side.

Writing of her first few days with Helen, Sullivan stated, "The greatest problem I shall have to solve is how to discipline and control her without breaking her spirit. . . . I shall insist on reasonable obedience from the start."[18]

Helen was anything but obedient with her teacher. After one of Sullivan's attempts to discipline the child, Helen became furious and attacked her, knocking out one of Sullivan's front teeth.

Sullivan's stubborn, fiery temperament was now being put to the test and she refused to yield. She had been hired to do a job and she would make every attempt to do it. The first thing she intended to teach Helen was how to communicate with words.

Beyond Dreams

Almost from the moment of her arrival, Sullivan had been moving her fingers against Helen's palm, spelling words to her through manual sign language.

Sullivan spelled *d-o-l-l* when she presented Helen with the doll that the students at Perkins had bought for her. Helen was able to mimic the finger movements but could not understand their purpose. She had no understanding of spelling or even the concept of words.

That first spelling session ended badly. When Sullivan momentarily removed the doll, Helen believed it was being taken away for good, and she threw a tantrum.[1] To distract her, Sullivan switched to another word. She gave Helen a piece of cake and spelled *c-a-k-e* into her hand. Again, Helen imitated the finger motions but had no idea what they meant. She became distraught, and Sullivan was forced to end the session, letting the child have both the cake and the doll.[2]

It was to be the first of Sullivan's many struggles with Helen. In addition to educating her pupil, wrote Helen later, "Teacher had all the cares that most parents have to make their children wash behind their ears, comb and brush their hair, and put on clean clothes. That took a long time, as Helen . . . disliked being continually 'set to rights.' She was an incorrigible imp."[3]

The breakfast table became the scene of one of the most grueling battles Sullivan was to engage in with her new student. Since losing her sight and hearing, Helen had been allowed to wander around the table at mealtime using her fingers to pick food from her family's plates. Sullivan was shocked by this and refused to tolerate it when breakfast was served one morning shortly after her arrival. Helen flew into a rage, and Sullivan asked the Kellers—who had not finished their meal—to leave the room. She then locked the door and continued eating while Helen threw herself on the floor, kicking, shrieking, and attempting to pull Sullivan's chair out from under her.

Sullivan managed to remain seated. Eventually, Helen grew curious and got off the floor to find out what her teacher was doing. Sullivan allowed Helen to stand near her to discover that she was eating, but she refused to let Helen put her fingers in the plate.

"She pinched me, and I slapped her every time she

did it," Sullivan stated. "Then she went all around the table to see who was there, and finding no one but me, she seemed bewildered."[4]

The battle continued.

Helen took her seat and began to eat her breakfast with her fingers. Sullivan handed her a spoon. Helen promptly threw it on the floor. Sullivan forced Helen to pick up the spoon and get back in her chair. She put the spoon in the child's hand and guided her in scooping up food and placing it into her mouth. Soon, Helen was using the spoon by herself. Teacher and student finished the meal in peace, but another struggle erupted when Sullivan insisted that Helen fold her napkin.

"She threw it on the floor and ran toward the door," said Sullivan. "Finding it locked, she began to kick and scream all over again. It was another hour before I succeeded in getting her napkin folded."[5]

Sullivan finally sent Helen outside to play, then went up to her room, flung herself on the bed, and sobbed.

"I saw clearly that it was useless to try to teach her language or anything else until she learned to obey me," she wrote.[6]

Sullivan's task was complicated by the fact that the Kellers often interfered in these battles with Helen. Captain Keller, in particular, hated to see his daughter cry. Sullivan knew she needed to get Helen away from her family if she was ever to learn discipline.

She suggested to the Kellers that she live alone with Helen for a time. Sullivan was pleasantly surprised when Captain Keller offered her the use of the little cottage where Helen had been born. It was close to the main house.

The plan was quickly put into action. To ensure that Helen would not know where she was, the child was taken for a long drive before being brought to the cottage. Also, the furniture had been rearranged so the two rooms would not be familiar to Helen. Meals were brought over to the cottage and the Kellers were allowed to see Helen every day, though they were not allowed to let her know they were there.

Helen made it clear from the start that she was not happy about being alone with her teacher. She threw tantrums and refused to let Sullivan touch her.

Alone with Helen in this little cottage for two weeks, Annie Sullivan was determined to teach her spoiled new pupil to obey. Only then could the real lessons begin.

She spent much of her time standing near the door, obviously homesick.

Sullivan continued to enforce certain rules of behavior. She made Helen understand that she could not have breakfast until she was dressed. When Captain Keller peered through the window one morning at ten o'clock, he saw his daughter sitting miserably on the floor in her nightgown. Considerably upset, he commented that he had "a good mind to send that Yankee girl back to Boston."[7]

Helen and her teacher remained alone in the cottage for about two weeks. By March 20, 1887, Sullivan had encouraging news to report. Helen was settling down, doing daily exercises, and learning how to sew and crochet. After crocheting a long chain of red wool that stretched from one end of the room to the other, Helen patted herself on the arm and rubbed the wool against her cheek. She now wore a serene expression on her face and even allowed Sullivan to kiss her.

"The little savage has learned her first lesson in obedience, and finds the yoke easy," wrote Sullivan.[8]

It is not entirely clear what caused this change in the previously spoiled and headstrong child. Sullivan did acknowledge that she occasionally whipped Helen if she misbehaved. Yet the worst punishment she could inflict on her student was to refuse to "talk" to her. Although Helen was still unclear as to the meaning of the finger movements, she innately sensed they were her link to the outside world. Without Sullivan spelling into her hand, Helen felt as if she were isolated from the world.[9]

The change in Helen was obvious to her family. Now when Captain Keller looked through the window, he saw his daughter happily stringing beads or playing with a sewing card.

On one occasion, Captain Keller brought the family's dog, Belle, over to the cottage to visit Helen. Helen was giving her doll a bath at the time, but she suddenly sniffed the air and then tossed the doll into the washbowl as she felt around the room. When Helen came upon Belle, she hugged the setter and then began to manipulate her paws.

Puzzled at first, Sullivan noticed Helen form the letters *d-o-l-l*. She was teaching the dog to spell.

Moving back to the family house, Sullivan taught the Kellers the manual alphabet. She also had their assurance that they would not interfere with her attempts to discipline Helen.

By March 31, Helen knew eighteen nouns and three verbs. She was even requesting words on her own. It was when Helen had trouble differentiating between *mug* and *milk* that Sullivan took her outside to the water pump and spelled *w-a-t-e-r* as the water flowed over Helen's hand. On that day, April 5, 1887, Helen understood the meaning of language; she realized the manual alphabet was the key to everything she wanted or needed to know. She would later call that day "my soul's birthday."[10]

Now that Helen understood the connection between her teacher's finger movements and the words they represented, she began to explore the world eagerly with her hands. Sullivan was always by her side, tirelessly spelling throughout the day.

Whether they were visiting horses, going to the water pump, or seeing the turkeys and chickens, Sullivan spelled into Helen's hand.

Her ideas on teaching language to a deaf and blind child were based on the same principles by which a hearing child learns language. A child with normal hearing has been listening to language from parents, caretakers, and others for thousands of hours by the time he or she begins using recognizable words.[11] Sullivan communicated with Helen constantly, using complete sentences as she spelled into the child's hand. Just as a hearing child does not initially understand what is being said, it took time before Helen could comprehend most of what Sullivan was telling her.

Abstract ideas—as opposed to objects Helen could touch—were especially difficult for her to understand. Years later, she recalled the first time she grasped an abstract idea, while she was stringing beads of different sizes into various patterns.

"I had made many mistakes," she stated, "and Miss Sullivan had pointed them out again and again with gentle patience. Finally I noticed a very obvious error in the sequence and for an instant I concentrated my attention on the lesson and tried to think how I should have arranged the beads. Miss Sullivan touched my forehead and spelled with decided emphasis 'think.' In a flash I knew that that word was the name of the process that was going on in my head."[12]

Sullivan made sure Helen was informed of all experiences and conversations that were taking place around her. In this way, Helen became familiar with idioms and common expressions.

Helen was soon able to understand adjectives and adverbs as easily as she understood nouns. Before the arrival of Sullivan, Helen would indicate *small* by taking the thumb and index finger of one hand and pinching a small bit of the skin of the other hand. When she wanted to indicate *large*, she would spread all her fingers as widely as possible and then position them as if she were holding a large ball. When Sullivan substituted the actual words *small* and *large* for these signs, Helen immediately incorporated the words into her vocabulary.

Sullivan believed in allowing Helen to make mistakes when she used the manual alphabet, mixing up nouns and verbs just as a hearing child might. Sullivan would occasionally suggest a word or a sentence, but generally she simply wanted to encourage Helen's desire to communicate.

Helen did not need much encouragement; her days were filled with a variety of experiences. Student and teacher took long walks where Helen learned to distinguish flowers by feeling their stems and petals. She caught butterflies and tadpoles and ran her hands over the bodies of animals in the woods in order to learn what they were like. She felt a baby chick pecking its way out of the shell and touched the wings of a pigeon. At the circus, she was allowed to ride an elephant, hug a young lion, feel a giraffe's ears, and shake hands with a bear.

Helen began spelling from the moment she woke up in the morning and she did not stop throughout

Understanding language opened up the world to Helen, and she "talked" excitedly all day long. Here Jumbo, her pet Irish setter, sits patiently as Helen spells words into his paw.

the day. The times when Sullivan was not talking to her, Helen spelled into her own hand, carrying on entire conversations.

Understanding language opened up the world to Helen, and an inner happiness was clearly visible on her face. She learned how to laugh again, something she had rarely done since losing her hearing. One day, Sullivan was laughing as she approached Helen and she put the child's hand to her face while she spelled *l-a-u-g-h*. Then she tickled Helen until she began laughing and was as joyful as her teacher.[13]

Sullivan was, in fact, extremely happy. Helen's

loving nature and her dependency on her teacher filled a void in Sullivan's life. She had known nothing but loneliness since the death of her brother Jimmie in the Tewksbury poorhouse. Now there was Helen.

Sullivan could also lay to rest the fears that she would not be successful at teaching a deaf and blind child. Intelligent, curious, and thriving under her teacher's excellent guidance, Helen was making progress that was nothing short of remarkable.

Within several months of her arrival, Sullivan wrote, "Something within me tells me I shall succeed beyond all my dreams."[14]

Reading, Writing, and 'Rithmetic

"I must learn many things," Helen once declared.[1]

She did learn many things, and it seemed that now that the door to language was open to her, Helen must learn them as quickly as possible. Sullivan often felt that Helen was trying to make up for the first few years of her life, when she had been locked in a world of silent darkness.

Only a few months after the arrival of her teacher, Helen was running her fingertips over the raised letters of books Sullivan had borrowed from the Perkins school. She was learning to read.

Sullivan taught her student how to use these books by first spelling each letter into Helen's hand and then pressing the child's fingers onto a piece of cardboard that contained the embossed letter. It took Helen only one day to learn to read the entire alphabet as well as to recognize any word she already knew.

Sullivan made up a list of words familiar to Helen and asked Anagnos if he would have them printed in blocks. Helen had been using a special frame to hold embossed words; the frame allowed her to arrange the words into simple sentences. When the new words arrived from Anagnos, Helen immediately placed them in her frame and began putting together sentences.

Reading soon led to writing, and Helen learned a style called *square-hand*. The letters were similar to square-shaped letters found on today's digital displays. She kept her lines straight by placing her paper over a grooved board; the horizontal grooves corresponded to lines. It was a two-handed process for Helen. Her right hand guided the pencil; her left hand made sure the letters were the correct shape.

When Helen took a trip with her father to Huntsville, Alabama, that summer of 1887, she wrote a letter to her mother:

> *Helen will write mother letter papa did give helen medicine mildred did sit in swing mildred will kiss helen teacher did give helen peach george is sick in bed george arm is hurt anna did give helen lemonade dog did stand up conductor did punch ticket papa did give helen drink of water in car carlotta did give helen flowers anna will buy helen pretty new hat helen will hug and kiss mother helen will come home grandmother does love helen*
> *good-by*[2]

Sullivan periodically wrote to Anagnos, informing him of Helen's development. He noted that it had taken Helen only four months to acquire the same amount of knowledge that Laura Bridgman had taken two years to learn.[3]

But the swift pace at which Helen was learning had its price. Her appetite began to diminish that summer and she was experiencing sleepless nights. When the family doctor was called in, he claimed that the seven-year-old Helen had a mind that was too active. He also complained—as many individuals would throughout Helen's life—that she was being overworked by her teacher. Sullivan was, in fact, a perfectionist. She made Helen write letters over and over until there was not a single mistake. It became an exhausting ordeal under Sullivan's guidance.[4]

The demand for perfection also took its toll on Sullivan. Her eyes were inflamed and aching and she suffered from insomnia. Yet there seemed to be no way to curb Helen's desire to learn.

Helen's appetite returned eventually, and Sullivan began teaching her Braille. Invented by Louis Braille, a blind French boy, the Braille alphabet is based on a system of six raised dots that blind people read with their fingertips. (There are also Braille codes for music and mathematics.) To write Braille, a pencil-like stylus is used to push dots down into heavy paper that sits in a pocket-size frame, called a slate. The paper is then turned over, and the embossed dots can be read by touching them with the fingertips.

Although the Braille method of writing was at first slower than Helen's square-hand script, she preferred it because now she could read what she wrote. Learning Braille also made more books available to Helen. She read with two hands. The index finger of her left hand followed the lines in the book, while her right hand spelled out the words manually—just as a child who can see and hear might read aloud to himself.

Christmas that year was a very special occasion in the Keller house. Helen was no longer a wild monster who ran around disrupting the household with fits of rage. She was well behaved and she could communicate.

"Miss Annie, I thank God every day of my life for sending you to us," said Kate Keller.[5]

Helen's accomplishments were turning her into a celebrity. In 1888, Anagnos at the Perkins Institution published a report called "Helen Keller: A Second Laura Bridgman." He wrote that Helen's achievements surpassed Bridgman's and he called Helen an intellectual phenomenon. Soon people across the country—and eventually throughout the world—believed Helen was capable of just about anything, including such exaggerated claims as speaking fluently, performing on the piano, and solving geometry problems.

The world seemed to take note of every event in Helen's life.

When Helen was ten, her dog, Lioness, was accidentally shot by a policeman. Money, as well as offers of other dogs, poured in from across the United States and Europe. Helen accepted the money, but not for the purchase of another dog. She chose instead to use it to help send Tommy Stringer, a deaf, mute, and

When she first learned to read, Helen used both hands. With one, she traced the Braille dots in the book. With the other, she finger-spelled the words. This was her way of reading aloud to herself.

blind boy, to the Perkins Institution. She also wrote personal letters and newspaper articles to help finance his education.

Shortly after Anagnos wrote his report, he traveled to Alabama and invited Helen, her mother, and her teacher to visit the Perkins school—free of charge—for several months.

Always eager to put her thoughts on paper, Helen wrote to the Perkins students:

> *Helen will write little blind girls a letter Helen and teacher will come to see little blind girls . . . Helen and blind girls will have fun blind girls can talk on fingers Helen will go to school with blind girls . . . Helen is tired Helen will put letter in envelope for blind girls.*[6]

The journey was made in May 1888. Helen, Anne Sullivan, and Kate Keller headed north, stopping in Washington, D.C., to visit Alexander Graham Bell. Bell enjoyed visiting with Helen and was extremely interested in the teaching methods used by Sullivan. Although Sullivan said she did not have any specific teaching methods, she felt strongly about avoiding the traditional form of education, where children sat indoors at a table, obeying the teacher's instructions. Much of Sullivan's time with Helen was spent outdoors, experiencing nature firsthand and often allowing Helen's questions to direct the day's lesson.

"A boat on the Tennesse [sic] river, the barnyard, the circus, the village store were our playgrounds," Helen wrote years later. "They supplied me with an enormous amount of knowledge and education. All out of doors was a museum of object lessons."[7]

While in Washington, Helen, Anne Sullivan, and Kate Keller met President Grover Cleveland. They then traveled on to Boston, arriving there on May 26.

They attended the graduation exercises at Perkins, with Helen and Sullivan sitting on the platform next to Laura Bridgman. At the ceremony, Helen read a poem with one hand while spelling it in the air with the other. Sullivan served as the translator for the audience. Helen was—and always would be—a dynamic performer on stage, easily drawing in the crowd with her attractive, animated features and luminous expression. Many people in the audience wept because they were so moved by her performance.

Helen spent time with the Perkins students learning beadwork, knitting, and modeling clay until school closed for the summer. Then the trio moved on to Cape Cod, Massachusetts. Helen loved the beach and ran toward the ocean fearlessly. She was tossed under a wave, and when she emerged, Helen calmed herself down to ask her teacher, "Who put salt in the water?"[8]

September and October were spent back at the Perkins school, where Helen begged Anagnos—who was Greek—to teach her the Greek language. Sullivan had already taught her some French and Helen enjoyed practicing her foreign-language skills.

She wrote in a letter: "*Mon cher Monsieur Anagnos* . . . When I go to France I will talk French. A little French boy will say, *Parlez-vous Français?* and I will

In 1888, Helen was invited to spend a few months studying at the Perkins Institution for the Blind, above.

say, *Oui, Monsieur, vous avez un joli chapeau. Donnez moi un baiser.*[9]

Helen was back home by December and began studying arithmetic, geography, zoology, and reading. But Sullivan's eyes continued to bother her and often the lessons had to be interrupted. It was soon obvious that Sullivan would require further medical treatment on her eyes, and during the summer of 1889 teacher and student were separated for the first time in two years.

A companion from Perkins was hired to care for Helen while Sullivan traveled to Boston for three and a half months. In the one letter that is available from this time, Helen wrote to her teacher: "I do want you to come to me soon. I miss you so very, very, very much. I cannot know about many things when my dear teacher is not here."[10]

By the fall, Helen and Sullivan were together again, and they returned to the Perkins Institution. Sullivan continued to teach her student, but Helen also took classes from Perkins teachers in basketry, clay modeling, and music. Helen enjoyed music— particularly the piano—and would become familiar with many musical compositions as an adult.

"I enjoy the music of the piano most when I touch the instrument," she later wrote. "If I keep my hand on the piano-case, I detect tiny quavers, returns of melody, and the hush that follows."[11]

With one hand on the piano, she would wave the other through the air, keeping perfect time to the music.[12]

Helen also studied French in earnest during this time, and although she was only nine years old, she mastered the language within three months.

But written language was not enough to satisfy Helen's insatiable desire to learn. One of Laura Bridgman's former teachers had met Ragnhild Kaata of Norway. Like Helen, Ragnhild was deaf and blind. Unlike Helen, she could speak.

When Helen learned of this, she spelled to Sullivan, "I must speak."[13]

Helen traveled with Sullivan in March of 1890 to see Sarah Fuller, principal of the Horace Mann School for the Deaf in Boston. The lesson began immediately.

"She passed my hand lightly over her face, and let me feel the position of her tongue and lips when she

Michael Anagnos, right, director of the Perkins Institution, was so impressed with Helen that he published a report about her.

made a sound," Helen later recalled. "I was eager to imitate every motion and in an hour had learned six elements of speech: *M, P, A, S, T, I.* I shall never forget the surprise and delight I felt when I uttered my first connected sentence: 'It is warm.'"[14]

Proud as Helen was of her accomplishment, her speech was very hard to understand. Later, she realized she should have first strengthened and developed her vocal organs—which were not accustomed to being used—before trying to articulate sounds.

But that did not stop her from trying. Once Helen's lessons with Fuller ended, Sullivan took over and the two practiced tirelessly. Helen would place her fingers in Sullivan's mouth, reaching deep into her teacher's throat. Sullivan would often gag, but there was never a question of giving up.

Helen was never able to achieve natural pitch or volume, and she frightened the local dogs and horses when practicing her speech outdoors, according to a neighbor. But Helen was joyful about being able to pronounce sounds. She talked constantly to Sullivan, in hopes of improving her speech.

"Last evening I went out into the yard and spoke to the moon," Helen wrote to Sarah Fuller. "I said, 'O moon, come to me.' Do you think the lovely moon was glad that I could speak to her?"[15]

6

Put to the Test

Helen had been fluent with language for only three years when she wrote a story. Using her Braille slate, eleven-year-old Helen wrote a fairy tale called "The Frost King" and sent it to Michael Anagnos on November 4, 1891, as a birthday gift.

Anagnos was thrilled. He had the story printed in *The Mentor*, Perkins's alumni magazine, and it also appeared in *The Goodson Gazette*, a weekly publication of the Virginia Institution for the Education of the Deaf and Dumb and Blind. The editors of the *Gazette* called the story "without parallel in the history of literature."[1]

But a week later, the fairy tale became the focus of one of the most controversial and distressing episodes in Helen's life.

It was discovered that "The Frost King" was very similar to another story, called "The Frost Fairies," written by Margaret T. Canby in her book *Birdie and His Friends*. The *Gazette* ran Helen's story next to Canby's, showing the many phrases and paragraphs that were identical.

Helen was brought before a committee of Perkins officials—including Anagnos—and questioned about the story. Devastated at being considered a fraud, Helen said she did not recall ever being told the story "The Frost Fairies." She thought what she wrote was original. A vote was taken on whether or not Helen was guilty of plagiarism—did she copy someone else's story and claim it as her own? Anagnos broke the four–four tie by voting in favor of her innocence.

Sullivan's explanation was that Helen had Canby's book read to her during the summer of 1888 when she stayed at Sophia C. Hopkins's house on Cape Cod. Helen had spent time alone with Hopkins while Sullivan received medical treatment for her eyes. Hopkins, a close friend of Sullivan's, read numerous books to Helen and, according to Sullivan, recalled reading stories from Canby's *Birdie and His Friends*.[2]

Helen possessed an extraordinary memory. It seemed plausible that she might have retained sentences and images from the story without specifically remembering "The Frost Fairies."

"Even now," she wrote later, "I cannot be quite sure of the boundary line between my ideas and those I find in books."[3]

Canby herself wrote a kind letter to Helen, saying

she was pleased Helen had enjoyed the story. But Helen never completely recovered from the incident.

"I have never played with words again for the mere pleasure of the game," she wrote. "Indeed, I have ever since been tortured by the fear that what I write is not my own."[4]

Even writing letters to her mother became difficult for Helen. She would work on sentences over and over again, wanting to ensure that she had not previously read the words elsewhere.

Helen's self-confidence was not the only thing damaged by the incident. The relationship she and Sullivan had enjoyed with Anagnos came to an end. Although the Perkins director had voted in favor of Helen's innocence, he soon began telling people she was "a living lie."[5] Helen and Sullivan left the Perkins school; they had no desire to return.

Back in Tuscumbia, where Helen had a new baby brother, Phillips, the two were tired and depressed. Sullivan stopped regular lessons for a time and encouraged Helen to write a short account of her life for *Youth's Companion*. She thought it might help restore Helen's self-confidence.

"I wrote timidly, fearfully, but resolutely, urged on by my teacher, who knew that if I persevered, I should find my mental foothold again and get a grip on my faculties," Helen wrote later.[6]

During 1893, Helen and her teacher traveled to Washington, D.C., for President Cleveland's second inauguration. They also visited Niagara Falls in New York and the Chicago World's Fair. Alexander Graham Bell guided Helen around the World's Fair; he had been one of Helen's strongest supporters during the "Frost King" incident. Attracting a lot of attention wherever she went, Helen was allowed to touch all the exhibits at the fair, including diamonds from the Cape of Good Hope, in South Africa, and rare works of art.

Bell was among the many supporters Helen would have throughout her life. She was often dependent on them to pay her expenses. Men such as John S. Spaulding, owner of a Boston sugar company, and philanthropist William Wade gave money to Helen and her teacher. It was used to cover the cost of Helen's education as well as travel expenses. Sullivan had not received her salary for a long time and money was always in short supply.

Their financial situation was not helped by the fact that Captain Keller had lost his job as district marshal a few years earlier. The Keller funds were so low that Captain Keller decided to have Helen appear in a vaudeville show, where she would be paid $500 a week to stand on stage in front of large audiences. Kate Keller vehemently refused to allow her daughter to be used as an exhibition, and the idea was dropped.

The following year, Helen began attending the Wright-Humason School for the Deaf in New York City, which focused on teaching speech to the deaf. Studying geography, French, German, and arithmetic, Helen especially hoped to improve her voice and lip-reading skills. One of her classmates recalled how Helen could read the words written on the blackboard by using her fingers to trace the chalk marks. She was also able to play checkers with the students on a specially built board. She went bobsledding in

*Helen's accomplishments were turning her into a celebrity.
The world seemed to take note of every event in her life.*

Central Park, took horseback-riding lessons, and performed in the school play.

Helen enjoyed her time at the school. While her articulation improved, it soon became clear that her voice would never sound like everyone else's. Yet Helen continued working. She met such celebrated people as John D. Rockefeller, Woodrow Wilson, and author Mark Twain, who became a very close friend.

On August 19, 1896, while Helen was in her second year at the school, her father died in Tuscumbia. Helen's sorrow was eased by her new religion, Swedenborgianism. Based on the writings of the eighteenth-century Swedish scientist and philosopher Emanuel Swedenborg, the religion promised an after-life where people did not suffer from handicaps or limitations. Helen had been introduced to the religion by Alexander Graham Bell's secretary, John Hitz. Although her father had been a Presbyterian and her mother an Episcopalian, Helen would consider herself a Swedenborgianist all her life.

Helen's education continued with her enrollment in the Cambridge School for Young Ladies in October 1896. Located in Cambridge, Massachusetts, the school would prepare Helen for Radcliffe College, the women's school associated with Harvard, also in Cambridge.

Although she would now be competing with girls who could hear and see, Helen was not frightened by the obstacles. "The thought of going to college took root in my heart and became an earnest desire," she wrote.[7]

It was originally determined that it would take

Helen five years to complete the course of study at the Cambridge School, which Helen's sister, Mildred, also began attending. By the end of Helen's first year, it appeared that she could finish in only three more years. Arthur Gilman, who headed the school, was amazed at Helen's enthusiasm for learning, which always kept her well ahead of her lessons. To Helen, "Difficulties were merely new heights to be scaled," Gilman wrote.[8]

Since few books could be found in Braille, Sullivan had to read everything Helen was required to learn, and then pass on the information to her student. Yet Gilman observed that there was "little difference between the treatment of Helen and the other pupils. Miss Sullivan sat at Helen's side in the classes, interpreting to her with infinite patience the instructions of every teacher."[9]

Helen was allowed to take part of her examinations for entrance to college. Gilman, who had learned the manual alphabet, translated the exam questions for Helen so that no one could accuse Sullivan of helping her. While the students at the school wrote their answers in longhand, Helen was allowed to type her answers on a typewriter. She was given a slightly longer period of time in which to take the exam to make up for the slow pace of Gilman's translations. He was not as fluent in the use of the manual alphabet as Sullivan.

Helen passed all her subjects, which included elementary and advanced German, French, Latin, English, and Greek and Roman history. In English and German, she received honors. A typical question

With her fingers, Helen could read her teacher's lips. Sullivan served as Helen's eyes and ears to the world.

Helen was asked on her exams was "Where are the following: Arbela, Coryere, Dacia, Lade, Rubicon, Trasimene; and with what famous event is each connected?"[10]

With part of the college entrance examinations behind them, Sullivan decided that Helen could complete her education at the Cambridge School in only two more years. The following year, however, Helen's grades were not good. The necessary Braille textbooks were delayed in arriving from England, and math—especially geometry—had always been hard for Helen. Since she could not see the geometric figures on the blackboard, Helen made the shapes out of straight and curved wires.

"It takes me a long time to prepare my lessons, because I have to have every word of them spelled out in my hand," Helen wrote in December 1896. "Not one of the textbooks which I am obliged to use is in raised print; so of course my work is harder than it would be if I could read my lessons over by myself. . . . Sometimes it really seems as if the task which we have set ourselves were more than we can accomplish; but at other times I enjoy my work more than I can say."[11]

Although Gilman reluctantly agreed to the new, shorter schedule for Helen's schooling, he believed Helen was being overworked and even called Sullivan's treatment of her "cruel."[12] He wrote many letters to Kate Keller, suggesting that Sullivan be removed as Helen's companion and that he be appointed as Helen's guardian.

Alarmed by Gilman's reports that her daughter

was close to collapsing from working too hard, Kate Keller sent a telegram to Gilman in December 1897, agreeing to make him Helen's guardian. Sullivan, however, found a letter Gilman was about to mail to Kate Keller. She tore open the envelope, read the letter, and became furious when she realized that she was to be removed from Helen. It was Sullivan's belief that Gilman wanted to keep Helen at his school merely because of the favorable publicity she brought to it.[13]

She told her student, "Helen, I fear we are going to be separated!"

Helen responded, "What! Separated? What do you mean?"[14] Extremely upset at the thought of losing her teacher, Helen refused to eat or sleep. Sullivan quickly sent a three-word telegram to Kate Keller: "We need you."

Kate Keller traveled to Massachusetts and immediately changed her mind. She told Helen she would not fire Sullivan. Both Helen and Mildred were removed from the school. Mildred returned to Tuscumbia with her mother, and Helen was tutored privately in Wrentham, Massachusetts, under Merton S. Keith.

"I find I get on faster, and do better work with Mr. Keith than I did in the classes at the Cambridge School," Helen wrote in April 1898, "and I think it was well that I gave up that kind of work. . . . I have accomplished more, and been happier than I could have been there."[15]

By the fall of 1900, at the age of twenty, Helen Keller was ready to enter college.

7

Higher Education

Helen Keller was set on going to Radcliffe for one simple reason: The college did not want her.[1]

Radcliffe's dean, Agnes Irwin, believed there were too many difficulties in teaching Keller, since Sullivan would have to translate all the course work—books and lectures—through the manual alphabet.

A determined Keller wrote to the chairman of the college's academic board on May 5, 1900: "I realize that the obstacles in the way of my receiving a college education are very great—to others they may seem insurmountable; but, dear Sir, a true soldier does not acknowledge defeat before the battle."[2]

Keller was, in fact, heading down a path that relatively few women at that time had followed. During the Victorian period—1837 to 1901—a woman was expected to devote herself to marriage and family; comforting her husband after his hard day of work, dedicating herself to bringing up their children properly, and creating a peaceful home environment.[3]

There were, however, opportunities for women interested in attending college, and those opportunities were on the rise. In 1870, women made up one-fifth of all college and university students; by 1900, they constituted more than one-third.[4] Still, any woman at the turn of the century who had received a college education was considered nothing less than a pioneer.[5]

Many of Keller's friends were against the idea of her attending college, believing it to be "madness."[6] They encouraged her to head a school for the deaf and blind instead.

Not everyone supported that idea. Alexander Graham Bell thought it was extremely important that the twenty-year-old Keller stay in close contact with people who could hear and see. Heading a school for the deaf and blind, he argued, would restrict her. She would be in contact with disabled people only. The plan was eventually abandoned, and Keller later referred to it as an "attempt to divert me from my education."[7]

She began her freshman year at Radcliffe in September 1900. Her class consisted of about one hundred women, the largest class in the school's history.[8] Never before had one of the students been both blind and deaf.[9]

Keller was entering a college where she was not

Helen became close friends with the famous inventor Alexander Graham Bell, right, whose mother and wife were both deaf. Bell was very interested in the teaching methods used by Annie Sullivan, center.

wanted and where she would be expected to keep up with hearing and sighted students. Some people also questioned the practicality of her education, wondering what she would do with a college degree.

"But love of knowledge had stopped the ears with which I hear. . . . I realized that the avenues of usefulness opened to me were few and strait. But who shall set bounds to the aspirations of the mind?" Keller wrote.[10]

At Radcliffe, Sullivan sat by Keller's side in class, spelling the lectures into her hand. She also read most of Keller's textbooks to her since few were available in Braille. From the start, there was gossip at Radcliffe about which of these two women was really attending college.

"Why don't they say outright that Miss Sullivan is entering Radcliffe instead of Helen Keller, a blind, deaf and dumb girl," said one of the college's supervisors, repeating the talk that was going around the campus.[11]

But a considerable amount of work was left to Keller. She could not take notes because she needed her hands to "listen." After class, she would quickly return home and use her Braillewriter—similar to a typewriter except that it produced Braille rather than type—to record what she could remember of the lectures.

In spite of her outstanding memory, Keller had difficulty keeping up. She studied French, German, history, English composition, and English literature during her first year. In French and German, she read the works of many great writers, such as Racine and Goethe. Her history class ran from the fall of the

Roman Empire to the eighteenth century, a period spanning more than twelve hundred years.

The workload was heavier than Keller had imagined. There was no time now to enjoy the quiet of the evening or reflect on one's own thoughts. The hours of reading and studying were also difficult for Sullivan. Her eyesight became so bad that she could barely see past the end of her nose. For more than a year, Keller had been trying to persuade her teacher to take a rest. She had occasionally contemplated giving up the idea of attending college because of its effect on her teacher's eyes.

To make matters worse, Sullivan had been telling people she would kill herself if she went blind. A doctor was finally consulted. Hearing that Sullivan read as much as five hours a day, he advised her to rest her eyes completely.

But that was not possible because there was no one to take Sullivan's place. Keller did what she could to help. "When she [Sullivan] asked if I did not want certain passages reread, I lied and declared that I could recall them. As a matter of fact, they had slipped from my mind," Keller wrote.[12]

Keller also hid the fact that she herself was bothered by fatigue and headaches. She worried that Sullivan would again be accused of working her too hard.

Keller participated in many activities with the other students. Although she could not join field hockey or basketball, she swam, played chess and checkers, rode a tandem bicycle around Cambridge, and was voted vice president of her class. As a gift,

Keller's classmates bought her a Boston terrier, whom she named Phiz.

But there was also a sadness in Keller. College life made her painfully aware that she was not like the other students. She felt lonely when the girls forgot to greet her on the stairs or in classrooms.[13] Only one classmate learned the manual alphabet in order to communicate with her. The fact that Keller and her teacher were staying in a house on the outskirts of town further isolated Keller from the other girls, who all lived on campus.

"Sometimes, it is true, a sense of isolation enfolds me like a cold mist as I sit alone and wait at life's shut gate," she wrote. "Beyond there is light, and music, and sweet companionship; but I may not enter. Fate, silent, pitiless, bars the way."[14]

As always, Keller depended on Sullivan for assistance and companionship. The only time the two women were separated was when Keller took exams. Agnes Irwin personally paid for two proctors to administer Keller's exam questions, which she was allowed to answer on a typewriter.

During Keller's second year at Radcliffe, she began to write English compositions based on her life. Her English professor, Charles Townsend Copeland, encouraged Keller to write about her unique experiences, and he praised the results. Before long, editors at the *Ladies' Home Journal* learned about Keller's compositions. They invited her to write the story of her life, which they would publish in five monthly installments. The magazine was offering to pay $3,000 for her autobiography.

Keller had never been comfortable depending on wealthy friends for financial aid, and now she had an opportunity to support herself. But juggling schoolwork with writing a book proved too much for the two women; they needed help. A friend recommended John Macy. Twenty-five years old, Macy was an English instructor at Harvard and also an editor at *Youth's Companion*. He agreed to help Keller with the articles and quickly learned the manual alphabet so that he could work directly with her.

From the start, Macy was impressed by Keller's memory. "She remembered whole passages, some of which she had not seen for many weeks, and could tell, before Miss Sullivan had spelled into her hand a half-dozen words of the paragraphs under discussion, where they belonged and what sentences were necessary to make the connections clear," he said.[15]

With Macy's assistance the articles were expanded into a book, and *The Story of My Life* was published in March 1903. Although Sullivan did not want anything in the book about herself except what Keller had written, the editors knew that the public was as curious about Sullivan as they were about Keller.[16] As Mark Twain had written in a letter to Helen, "You are a wonderful creature, the most wonderful in the world—you and your other half together—Miss Sullivan, I mean, for it took the pair of you to make a complete and perfect whole."[17]

It was decided to include many of the letters Sullivan had written since first arriving in Tuscumbia. Also in the book was much of Keller's correspondence and an account of her education that

Macy had written. Dedicated to Alexander Graham Bell, the book has become a classic.

Macy continued to help Keller after the book's publication. To spare Sullivan's eyes, he assisted Keller with her studies, which were considerable. During her four years at Radcliffe, she took two courses in French, one in German, two in English

Learning geometry was especially hard for Helen. Here, she works out some geometry problems, using wires.

composition, one-half in John Milton (the seventeenth-century English writer), one in government, one in economics, one in history, two in Shakespeare, one in Elizabethan literature, one in English literature of the nineteenth century, one in the English Bible, and one in the history of philosophy. Each full course required her to attend three lectures a week for one year. The half-course required less.

She graduated *cum laude* (with honors) on June 28, 1904. She was the first deaf and blind person to earn a bachelor of arts degree. Her mother was too ill to attend the graduation ceremony, but several close friends were there to watch her receive her diploma. Keller was disappointed that Sullivan's name was not mentioned during the ceremony, and she recalled that the faculty did not speak to either of them.

"We had come in to our seats quietly that afternoon, and we went out as soon as we could, caught a street car and hastened away," she wrote."[18]

Keller and Sullivan now made their home in a farmhouse on seven acres of land in Wrentham. They had bought it for $2,700 just before Keller graduated. Shares of stock in Spaulding's sugar company were sold to pay for it.

Macy continued helping Keller with the magazine articles she wrote concerning the education of the blind and preventing blindness. He also acted as interpreter when she lectured.

"I cannot enumerate the helpful kindnesses with which he smoothed my paths," Keller stated. "Once, when I was tired with the manual labor of my copying, he sat up all night and typed forty pages of my manuscript, so that they might reach the press in time."[19]

Macy and Sullivan worked closely together, and they fell in love. Macy proposed marriage but it took Sullivan a year to consent. Keller worried that she was the obstacle standing in the way of the marriage.

"Oh, Teacher," she said, "if you love John, and let him go, I shall feel like a hideous accident."[20]

Sullivan insisted that Keller must approve the marriage before she would agree to it. Keller gave her approval, and the two were married on May 3, 1905, in the Wrentham farmhouse. During the couple's honeymoon to New Orleans, Keller stayed with her mother in Tuscumbia. When Sullivan and Macy returned, the three lived in the seventeen-room farmhouse.

Keller would later look back on those years in Wrentham as the best of her life. For the first time, she was able to take walks freely and by herself; Macy had set up a series of ropes and wire for a quarter of a mile along the property for her to hold on to. John Hitz, who had introduced Keller to Swedenborgianism, was a frequent visitor, and the two enjoyed taking long walks in the early morning. Hitz "stimulated in me the love of Nature that is so precious a part of the music in my silence and the light in my darkness," Keller wrote.[21]

In 1908, with John Macy's help, Keller wrote another book about her experiences, entitled *The World I Live In*. Based on a series of essays that had appeared in *Century* magazine, the book contained

Keller's descriptions of how she functioned without being able to see or hear.

"My world is built of touch-sensations, devoid of physical color and sound; but without color and sound it breathes and throbs with life . . . with my hands I can feel the comic as well as the beautiful," she wrote.[22]

She explained her reliance upon touch, taste, and particularly smell:

> *I have not, indeed, the all-knowing scent of the hound or the wild animal. . . . Nevertheless, human odors are as varied and capable of recognition as hands and faces. The dear odors of those I love are so definite, so unmistakable, that nothing can quite obliterate them. If many years should elapse before I saw an intimate friend again, I think I should recognize his odor instantly in the heart of Africa.[23]*

The book was a success with the public, and two years later Keller wrote an epic poem, "The Song of the Stone Wall." It told of her enjoyment in helping to build a stone wall around the Wrentham property.

Keller's books were selling well but she hesitated to write more. The public was interested in reading only about Keller's life, and she had grown tired of writing solely about herself. She was unsure of what to do next. She wrote:

> *I have received the best education my country can give me. Generous friends have assisted me and strewn my path with opportunities. The question now is, what shall I do with this education and these opportunities?[24]*

Causes

Determined to play an active role in life, Keller decided to work on behalf of the blind. She knew better than most people that there were numerous problems facing the blind. Many still lived in poorhouses such as the kind Sullivan had experienced as a child, and most did not have jobs or any kind of activity with which to occupy themselves.

Many blind people felt that they were of no use to their families and communities, and Keller herself often believed she was "a handicap, a hindrance, a tremendous burden."[1] She was a staunch supporter of training the blind—their minds and their hands. A blind person could not be considered hopeless as long as he had work to do and was able to read Braille.[2]

But that led to another problem.

There was no unified Braille system for the blind. One book might be printed in American Braille while another would use New York Point. Keller had learned five different types—American Braille, European Braille, New York Point, Moon Type, and Boston Line Type.

"The importance of a common embossed [raised] print is still more evident when we remember that one of the first things an adult person who loses his sight must do is to learn how to read and write by touch," she wrote. "He has to learn how to do the old thing in a new way, and that is hard enough without confusing him with a Babel of types."[3]

Keller would eventually tackle the issue of having one form of embossed type for the blind. In the meantime, she decided her first priority would be the prevention of blindness.

Keller was used to dealing with obstacles. But she now faced one that filled her with rage.

The major cause of blindness in infants was a condition called ophthalmia neonatorum. It was given to newborns by women infected with certain kinds of venereal disease—contagious diseases spread through sexual intercourse. Treating newborns with silver nitrate drops could prevent this blindness. But the subject was not one that was discussed openly. Women were never supposed to mention venereal disease; in fact, *no* properly brought up person at the turn of the twentieth century would ever talk about it.

Never one to shy away from a battle, Keller lashed out. "It is better that our sensibilities should be shocked than that we should be ignorant of facts," she said.[4]

She spoke at the annual convention of the American Association of Workers for the Blind, and she was appointed a member of the Massachusetts Commission for the Blind in 1906. She persuaded the editors of the *Kansas City Star* and the *Ladies' Home Journal* to print articles she wrote on the subject of preventing blindness in newborns.

Because of the recognition of her name and her aggressive efforts to educate the public, Keller's home was turned into a headquarters for information concerning the blind. According to John Macy, Keller was becoming more of an institution than a woman.[5] She was expected to advise and console everyone from mothers of blind infants to blind senior citizens whose lives were restricted to sitting idly at home. It was nearly impossible for her to keep up with all the mail, even with the help of Sullivan and Macy. Yet she continued to write articles, give lectures, and visit schools to promote the cause.

Busy as Keller was in her work for the blind, she was also being pulled in another direction. In 1909, she joined the Socialist Party of Massachusetts. Socialism is an economic system in which the public or the government—not the private individuals—controls the means of production. In England and France, for example, the government owns many industries, along with transportation facilities and public utilities. Macy was an ardent Socialist, and Keller had frequent contact with the stream of radical thinkers who visited the Wrentham farmhouse.

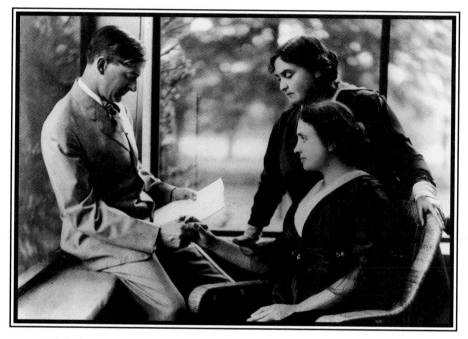

While helping Keller write the story of her life, editor John Macy, left, fell in love with Annie Sullivan, standing.

Keller later wrote a series of essays that discussed her Socialist views. According to her friend Van Wyck Brooks, the publication of this book of essays, *Out of the Dark* (1913), made Keller a social outcast for a while.

"She wrote that she had a red flag in her study, and, marching in suffrage parades, she shared the front page with baseball and the President's doings, accepting the notoriety and even happy in it when she felt that it brought Socialism to people's attention," Brooks wrote.[6]

The suffrage parades Brooks referred to were marches in support of women's right to vote. Keller was a strong supporter of the cause and wrote articles supporting it. "The dullest can see that a good many things are wrong with the world," she wrote in an article entitled "Why Men Need Woman Suffrage." "Perhaps one of the chief reasons for the present chaotic condition of things is that the world has been trying to get along with only half of itself. We see everywhere running to waste woman-force. . . ."[7]

While Keller's views were strong, they were not shared by Sullivan.

"She was not a woman suffragist, and I was," Keller wrote. "She was very conservative at that time. . . . The more we talked, the less we thought alike."[8]

Sullivan was equally doubtful about Keller's efforts on behalf of the blind. She did not believe the average blind person was capable of leading a full life.[9]

But the prevention of blindness and the education of the blind were causes to which Keller would devote much of her life. Although she considered loss of hearing more of a handicap than loss of sight, she did not work as hard for the deaf, for the simple reason that she could not do both at the same time.

In 1909, Keller met a singing instructor from the Boston Conservatory of Music. Charles A. White had devised a way for the deaf, mute, and blind to strengthen their vocal cords. Keller wanted to improve her speech so she could be more effective on the lecture circuit. Her voice had a tinny, robotlike quality to it. She hoped that lessons with White would make it sound more natural.[10]

White, a pleasant man who refused to be paid for

his voice lessons, began working with Keller the following year.[11] Learning the manual alphabet so he could communicate directly with his student, he initially focused his attention on Keller's breathing and pronunciation of vowels and consonants. In order to improve Keller's rhythm, he would tap her hand. Keller's task was to coordinate spoken words with the different rhythms of his taps.

She was able to achieve proper rhythm, but pitch—how high or low a sound is—was more difficult for her. She could not hear the difference in tones, but she could feel the vibrations in White's throat. Keller learned to match her voice to the different changes in pitch by keeping one hand on White's throat and the other on her own. Soon, Keller was able to imitate White when he sounded a tone and then raised it an octave higher.

Keller and White were eager to see the results of their work. Along with Sullivan, they attended a meeting of the American Association to Promote the Teaching of Speech to the Deaf. At the meeting, in Providence, Rhode Island, Keller gave a speech and recited a poem.

"I was told that many people understood me, even those who weren't used to the speech of the deaf!" Keller excitedly wrote to her mother. "It was the first time that I had ever spoken without being interpreted. It was the first time that Teacher had been able to sit and listen to me without feeling strained, anxious about my being understood."[12] Alexander Graham Bell, who was in the audience, claimed that he was astonished at the progress Helen had made.[13]

A later appearance, in January 1913, proved to be

Of all the arts, Keller most appreciated sculpture, which she could enjoy with her sense of touch.

a different experience for Keller. Onstage in Montclair, New Jersey, she was filled with stage fright. She lost control of her voice and could feel it rising higher with every word. Keller left the stage with tears pouring down her face.

She wrote of her lifelong struggle to speak clearly, "The pain and disappointment I have endured are incalculable, but they are a price worth paying for the joy I have in being able to keep this living bond between the outerworld and myself."[14]

In addition to her voice, there was another problem to which Keller turned her attention. Her left eye protruded; to hide that fact, nearly all the photographs taken of her up to this time were of her right profile. She had a surgeon operate on her, removing and replacing her eyes with glass ones. Most pictures taken after the operation show a full view of her face, with her eyes staring straight ahead.[15]

Keller now spent a considerable amount of her time lecturing. Sullivan would talk to the audience for an hour, explaining her teaching methods. Then it was Keller's turn. Either Kate Keller—who often accompanied her daughter on tour—or another companion would guide Keller to the stage, and she would demonstrate how she read lips by touching Sullivan's mouth with her fingers. The audience was invited to ask questions, which usually included: Do you close your eyes when you sleep? What is your idea of color? How was it possible for you to learn Greek? Can you tell the time of day without a watch?[16]

It was important that Keller and Sullivan go on lecture tours. Not only did they want to make the public aware of the problems facing the blind, but they also needed to earn money. Keller had finally agreed to accept financial help from the wealthy steel magnate Andrew Carnegie. But money was still in short supply because Keller's earnings also helped support Macy.

His marriage to Sullivan, however, was falling apart; he felt his wife spent too much of her time with Keller rather than with him.[17] Macy decided to sail alone to Europe in May 1913. The trip abroad was intended to give the couple some time apart. They hoped it would improve their relationship.

But when Macy returned four and a half months later, in the fall, he and Sullivan quarreled as furiously as ever. To make matters worse, he had begun drinking heavily.

The happy times in Wrentham had come to an end.

9

Loved Ones

"The happy light faded from Teacher's face, but she was too reserved to show her grief openly, and she refused to be comforted," Keller wrote of Sullivan's reaction to the breakup of her marriage. "To no one, except myself in the silence of the night, did she speak of her anguish or the terrible dreams that pursued her."[1]

The strain of the marriage dissolving, plus the constant travel that was required for the lectures, was affecting Sullivan's health. She was ill and exhausted nearly all the time. The year before, she had been hospitalized for a major operation and it had been uncertain whether she would survive.[2] Now in her midforties, Sullivan had gained a tremendous amount of weight, which caused further deterioration of her health.

"I really wonder that Teacher is able to go on," Keller wrote. "She is very, very tired, though she will NOT admit it. At times she trembles so much that we marvel when she gets through the lecture and nothing happens."[3]

In May 1914, Sullivan fell down some steps, painfully chipping her elbow. While the accident in itself was not serious, her failing eyesight was. Sullivan now needed to be guided when she walked or she would stumble.

Help was needed, and in the fall of that year a new person joined the household: Polly Thomson. The Scottish woman had never heard of Helen Keller, she did not know the manual alphabet, and she had no kind of literary skills. But Thomson could manage a household. She was able to keep a bank account in order—neither Keller nor Sullivan could do this—read a timetable without a ticket agent's help, and make schedules and itineraries for their travels. Often working without pay when money was scarce, Thomson became the eyes for both women, as well as the ears for Keller.[4] She would remain with Keller for the next forty-six years.

Another addition to the household was Peter Fagan, who acted as a secretary and assistant. A Socialist like Keller, Fagan was a colleague of Macy's. Fagan quickly learned the manual alphabet and Braille, and he accompanied Keller and Sullivan on a lecture tour to Chautauqua, New York, in 1916.

The tour was an enormous failure. As a pacifist,

Despite increasingly poor health and failing eyesight, Sullivan, standing, was a devoted companion. "I really wonder that Teacher is able to go on. She is very, very tired, though she will NOT admit it," worried Keller.

Keller did not believe in war and she spoke out against it. But the United States was preparing to enter World War I. The war had begun in Europe two years earlier and would eventually claim more than twenty million lives. No one was interested in Helen Keller's pacifist views. Sullivan sided with Keller against the war, and the two women returned to Wrentham after a few weeks, totally discouraged.

For Keller, the tour was particularly frustrating. "So long as I confine my activities to social service and the blind, they [the press] compliment me extravagantly, calling me the 'archpriestess of the sightless,' 'wonder woman,' and 'modern miracle,'" she wrote, "but when it comes to a discussion of a burning social or political issue, especially if I happen to be, as I so often am, on the unpopular side, the tone changes completely. . . . I do not object to harsh criticism so long as I am treated like a human being with a mind of her own."[5]

A cough that had been bothering Sullivan for some time was diagnosed as tuberculosis, and Sullivan was advised to spend the winter in Lake Placid, New York. Thomson would travel with Sullivan, while Keller was to accompany her mother to her sister's home in Montgomery, Alabama. Mildred was now married to Warren Tyson, and Kate Keller spent much of her time with her two daughters.

Separation from Sullivan was never easy for Keller. "I could not work, I could not think calmly. For the first time in my life it seemed folly to be alive," she wrote. "I had often been asked what I should do if anything happened to my teacher. I was now asking myself the same question . . . I was overwhelmed by a sense of my isolation."[6]

Peter Fagan changed everything.

He approached Keller in her study one night and expressed his love for her. Seven years younger than Keller, who was now in her midthirties, he proposed marriage, assuring Keller he would always be at her side to help her.

"His love was a bright sun that shone upon my helplessness and isolation," Keller wrote.[7]

Fagan knew Kate Keller did not like him, and he told Helen to keep their relationship a secret. They still managed to spend time together. Sometimes they took walks, or Fagan read to her. After the couple applied for a marriage license at the registrar's office in Boston, Keller decided to tell her mother.

But the story of the romance appeared in the newspapers before she had a chance to explain. When Kate Keller confronted her daughter, Helen denied everything. She was even taken north to see Sullivan, and again lied about the relationship. Kate Keller then threw Fagan out of the house, refusing to allow her daughter to say good-bye.

After a failed attempt by the couple to elope, Fagan still attempted to see Helen. But family members continued to intervene. One night, Helen waited on her sister's porch in Montgomery with a packed suitcase. She was obviously expecting to run off with Fagan, but he never showed up. The relationship was finally over.

Helen Keller described this time in her life as "a little island of joy surrounded by dark waters."

She wrote, "The love which had come, unseen and unexpected, departed with tempest on his wings."[8]

Keller later wrote that she was sure Anne Sullivan would have been sympathetic to the romance had she been nearby.[9]

But Sullivan, now fifty, was busy with her own concerns. She was tired, sick, and hated the cold weather of Lake Placid.[10] After seeing a newspaper advertisement for Puerto Rico, with its palm trees and sunny beaches, she headed south with Thomson.

Sullivan wrote that she was "happy and idle and aimless and pagan" in Puerto Rico and begged Keller to travel there with her mother.[11] But the Kellers never did. Sullivan and Thomson returned to Massachusetts in April 1917, only a few days after the United States declared war on Germany and entered the world war.

Helen Keller, Anne Sullivan, Polly Thomson, and Kate Keller did not stay long in the Wrentham farmhouse. It was too expensive to maintain, so the women traveled to Lake Placid, where Sullivan was told by a doctor that her test results had gotten mixed up with another patient's and she had never had tuberculosis after all. In the fall of 1917, Helen Keller, Sullivan, and Thomson purchased a small house in Forest Hills, New York. But first they would be spending several months in Hollywood, California.

Helen Keller was going to be in the movies.

In 1918, historian Francis Trevelyan Miller had suggested that a film be made of Keller's life. This was the age of silent films, and Keller and Sullivan were hopeful that *Deliverance* would earn a good deal of money. With Sullivan too ill and weak to travel during the past year, the women had not been able to go on lecture tours; they were nearly out of money.

Keller and Sullivan—who also appeared in the film—wanted the movie to be a completely accurate account of Keller's life. Instead, it was a combination of history and a considerable amount of fiction. Keller enjoyed her time in Hollywood, although acting was not easy for her.

"I was never quite at my ease when I posed," Keller wrote about the experience. "It was hard to be natural before the camera, and not to see it at that!"[12]

General directions were manually spelled into Keller's hand by Thomson. Signal taps guided her in performing various actions, such as walking toward a window, expressing surprise, or holding up her hands to the sun. When she was not acting, Keller enjoyed getting up at sunrise every morning to go horseback riding with Thomson. She was delighted to meet some famous actors of the day, such as Charlie Chaplin, Mary Pickford, and Douglas Fairbanks.

After they finished making the film, in December, the three women returned to Forest Hills. *Deliverance* opened in August 1919, but despite everyone's hopes, the film was a financial failure.

There was only one way left for Helen Keller to earn money, and it was a way that had outraged Kate Keller and Anne Sullivan nearly twenty-five years earlier. Helen would have to perform on the vaudeville circuit.

From 1920 through 1924, Keller and Sullivan traveled around the country earning more money

Keller was a popular speaker on issues of social service and the blind, but she was frustrated that her political views were often harshly criticized.

than they had ever made from books or lectures. Appearing alongside acrobats, monkeys, horses, dogs, and parrots, Keller and Sullivan opened in Mount Vernon, New York, to a sell-out crowd.

"My teacher was not happy in vaudeville," Keller wrote. "She could never get used to the rush, glare, and noise of the theatre; but I enjoyed it keenly."[13]

The act lasted twenty minutes and began with Sullivan describing Keller's achievements and her own role in Keller's life. Then the orchestra played as Keller came onto the stage. Sullivan took her hand and led her to the front. The audience was told about the memorable incident at the water pump when Keller learned the meaning of language, and they learned how Keller was able to speak. Keller then gave a short talk and the audience was allowed to ask questions.

Keller's inspirational message of hope and courage suited a nation that was recovering from World War I, and the act was a huge success. American poet Carl Sandburg wrote to her, "Dear Helen Keller, I saw and heard you last night and enjoyed it a thousand ways. . . . Those who see and hear you feel the zest for living, the zest you vibrate, is more important than any formula about how to live life."[14]

In 1921, shortly after the vaudeville tour began, Keller received news of her mother's death. She was devastated but had to go onstage two hours later to perform.[15]

By 1924, the vaudeville act had run its course. The story of Keller's life was unchanging; after an audience heard it once, they did not need to hear it again. In addition, the vaudeville lifestyle was simply too strenuous for Sullivan. Her eyes bothered her terribly because of the stage lights, and she developed first influenza and later bronchitis. Polly Thomson had taken Sullivan's place on stage during the last two years.

With vaudeville behind her, Keller began to look for a worthwhile cause to which she could devote herself. Meanwhile, Sullivan's deteriorating health continued to cast a shadow over their lives.

10

A Daring Adventure

Keller quickly found a way to put her talents and unique experiences to good use.

She and Sullivan were asked to raise money on behalf of the American Foundation for the Blind. The women were to travel from city to city, usually meeting in the private homes of wealthy individuals. At these meetings, Sullivan would again tell the story of Keller's life and how she had been educated. Then Keller would answer questions and ask for donations to the foundation.

The women were successful in their fund-raising efforts. Keller's story had a strong emotional appeal that always seemed to touch the audience. In October 1924, they signed a contract agreeing to help raise funds for the organization in exchange for a steady income. For the next three years, they visited 123 cities in the United States, speaking to a quarter of a million people.

By this time, Sullivan was nearly blind. She needed to rest, and Keller decided to take a leave of absence from the foundation. This would also allow her to write another book. Thomson went to Scotland for a vacation, and Sullivan and Keller stayed in Forest Hills. Before Thomson's return, Keller completed *My Religion*, an account of her belief in Swedenborgianism.

The book was a labor of love for Keller; Swedenborgianism was not only a religion to her, it was a way of life. "I cannot imagine myself without religion. I could as easily fancy a living body without a heart," she wrote. "To one who is deaf and blind, the spiritual world offers no difficulty. Nearly everything in the natural world is as vague, as remote from my senses as spiritual things seem to the minds of most people."[1]

As soon as the manuscript was sent to the publisher, she began *Midstream*, an autobiography of her years since attending college. The book picked up where *The Story of My Life* left off and was published in 1929.

In the spring of 1930, Keller, Sullivan, and Thomson traveled overseas and spent six months in Scotland, England, and Ireland. Sullivan was now sixty-four and in a general state of ill health. But the travel continued the following year when the women attended the first World Council for the Blind. They then went abroad again, visiting Brittany and

Yugoslavia, where Keller helped raise money for the blind.

The year 1931 was an important one for Keller. Because of her efforts, Braille had recently become accepted as the standard alphabet for the blind. A unified Braille code was established for English-speaking countries. No longer would a blind person in the United States or Great Britain have to be familiar with different systems of Braille. Also, Keller had successfully worked to get the United States Congress to pass a law calling for a national system of libraries for the blind to be established under the Library of Congress in Washington, D.C. This library system remains in effect today.

The women took another trip to England and Scotland in 1932 in hopes of improving Sullivan's health. Keller watched her teacher's condition deteriorate further after Sullivan learned of John Macy's death that August. Only fifty-five years old, Macy had died of a heart attack in Pennsylvania while on a lecture tour. Although Sullivan had been separated from her husband for nearly twenty years, she paid for the funeral.

Sullivan was now an invalid—emaciated, senile, and blind. After briefly entering a New York hospital in 1935, she made a short trip in the fall with Keller and Thomson to Jamaica, hoping the tropical beauty would revive her, as it had done when she stayed in Puerto Rico.

But it was too late.

Returning to New York in August, the women rented a cottage on Long Island near the ocean. "That was our desperate last effort to strengthen her so that her life might be tolerable," Keller wrote. "When someone tidied her room, she kept talking to me about the Angel of Death coming for her, and we should have everything in order at his arrival."[2]

Anne Sullivan, age seventy, died with Helen Keller holding her hand, on October 20, 1936.

When Keller reached out to touch Sullivan's face, she felt "fixed features from which expression had fled. I feel again the recoil, the cry that escaped me, 'It is not Teacher, it is not Teacher!'"[3]

The death of the woman who had been at her side for almost half a century plunged Keller into a state of loneliness and depression. "The wrench of separation from a beloved, unique, lifelong companion seems to have torn away an essential part of me," she wrote. "Deaf-blind a second time, I find any effort to speak cheerfully, to resume interest in a changed world . . . as hampering as sharp pain-throbs."[4]

The urn containing Sullivan's ashes was placed in a vault at the National Cathedral in Washington, D.C. She was the first woman to be offered this honor on the basis of her own achievements.

Keller needed to get away from the Forest Hills home that continually reminded her so much of Sullivan. Keller kept a diary as she traveled with Polly Thomson to England and then on to Scotland. Sullivan's absence was keenly felt. "Teacher had always journeyed with us through Britain. . . . She must be asleep, I thought, or she would be spelling into my hand the charm of light or color or flying cloud. . . . The yearning for her companionship almost unnerved me," she wrote.[5]

In Scotland, the two women stayed at the home of Thomson's brother, a minister. His children were able to use the manual alphabet, and their company cheered Keller. She loved children, just as her teacher had.

Returning home to Forest Hills, where she was surrounded by Sullivan's belongings, was difficult for Keller. A friend gave Keller a gift she had made—a sculpture of Sullivan's hand with the thumb and index fingers forming the letter *L* for *love*.

Keller and Thomson resumed traveling in April, heading for Japan. They gave ninety-seven lectures while visiting thirty-nine cities, and raised thirty-five million yen for the blind and deaf. The Japanese treated Keller like royalty, and as always Keller's speeches were filled with optimism and encouragement.

"We invite needless suffering when we entertain an exaggerated idea of our own suffering," she stated. "Instead of comparing our lot with that of those who are more fortunate than we are, we should compare it with the lot of the great majority of our fellow men. It then appears that we are among the privileged."[6]

In 1938, the diary Keller had been keeping since Sullivan's death was published as *Helen Keller's Journal*. Detailing Keller's grief over losing her teacher, it was the first of three books she would write without Sullivan's assistance.

Keller had Polly Thomson, of course, but Thomson was better at handling travel schedules and household affairs. She was not up to the task of working on Keller's manuscripts. Nella Braddy Henney, who had spent considerable time with Sullivan while writing the biography *Anne Sullivan Macy*, became Keller's editor and literary agent. She also became Keller's close friend; it was a friendship that would last nearly forty years.

Keller and Thomson sold the Forest Hills house in 1938 and moved to Connecticut. They named their new home Arcan Ridge, after a Scottish farm. The women owned eight dogs by this time, ranging from Helga, a Great Dane, to Et-Tu, a German shepherd that had failed as a Seeing Eye dog because of car sickness. Keller was the first person in the United States to own an Akita, a Japanese breed of dog, which was a gift from Japan's state department. Much as Keller loved dogs, the assortment of animals frequently got into fights and Thomson was often bitten when she intervened. Many of Keller's friends begged her to reduce the number of animals, but Keller refused.

World War II dominated the 1940s, and Keller spent much of her time visiting thousands of blind, deaf, and crippled soldiers. Visiting seventy army and navy hospitals over the course of a half year, Keller became the symbol of hope and courage.

"Face your deficiencies and acknowledge them; but do not let them master you," Keller stated. "Let them teach you patience, sweetness, insight. . . . When we do the best that we can, we never know what miracle is wrought in our life, or in the life of another."[7]

The soldiers responded instantly to Keller. Here was a woman who had spent her life feeling, she said, "like a music box with all the play shut up inside."[8]

She was living testimony to what she was saying. Aware of the soldiers' reaction to her, Keller called her visits to the hospitals "the crowning experience of my life."[9]

In 1946, Keller began touring for the American Foundation for the Overseas Blind, an organization closely associated with the American Foundation for the Blind. Through 1957, she traveled to thirty-five countries on five continents. Schools for the blind and deaf were often started as a result of her visits. Everywhere she went, Keller represented triumph over severe obstacles.

While Keller was visiting Rome in November 1946, Arcan Ridge burned to the ground because of an improperly functioning oil furnace. Keller had been working on a memoir of Sullivan and had written most of it, but the manuscript was destroyed along with many other irreplaceable letters, papers, and valuables. Keller refused to allow friends to raise money in her behalf. The only donations she would accept were those for the blind and the deaf. She would not accept anything for herself.

Two years later, Keller and Thomson traveled to Hiroshima, Japan, where an atomic bomb had been dropped on August 6, 1945, killing 90,000 people and wounding 150,000 more. With the city leveled and the survivors suffering, Keller became even more determined to fight for world peace.

She continued traveling around the world on

behalf of the blind, visiting Australia, South America, and many African countries. She was second only to First Lady Eleanor Roosevelt as the United States' most effective ambassador of goodwill.

During this tour, Polly Thomson suffered a minor stroke. The women had to return home to give Thomson a rest, but they headed back to Europe in 1950. Despite the fact that doctors had advised Thomson to lead a quieter life, Keller and Thomson

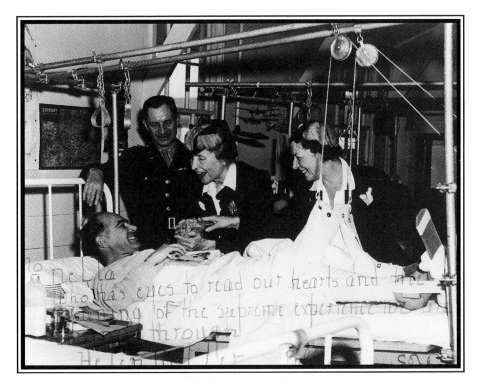

Keller traveled with Polly Thomson, right, bringing a message of hope and courage to thousands of blind, deaf, and crippled soldiers. She autographed this photo for her friend and editor Nella Braddy.

visited South Africa the following year, and then Egypt, Lebanon, Syria, Jordan, and Israel.

While the travel was exhausting for Thomson, the seventy-three-year-old Keller was still eager for new experiences. She again became the subject of a movie with the making of *The Unconquered*, a documentary of her life. The film included footage of Sullivan describing how Keller had been taught to speak, and a memorable scene of Keller moving with uplifted arms as she learned the art of dance from modern dance choreographer Martha Graham. Narrated by actress Katherine Cornell, the film won the Academy Award in 1955 for the best feature-length documentary. It would later be renamed *Helen Keller in Her Story*.

Keller continued working on her memoirs of Sullivan once the filming of the movie was completed. It was an upsetting task for Keller and she often found it difficult to sleep. But the book *Teacher* was published in 1955 and sold well. That same year, Keller was the first woman to receive an honorary degree from Harvard University. Radcliffe College gave her its alumnae achievement award, naming a garden after her and a fountain after Sullivan.

Keller was considered the greatest woman alive in the United States during this time.[10] Her home in Tuscumbia was placed on the National Register of Historic Places and made into a permanent local shrine. The play *The Miracle Worker* was written about the life of Helen Keller and her teacher and was broadcast on television in 1957. Two years later,

William Gibson's drama began a successful run on Broadway, and in 1962 it was made into a movie.

Thomson had become very possessive of Keller during these years, often isolating her from friends by forbidding her to socialize. In 1957, Thomson suffered another stroke. This left her unable to help with any of the housework or travel duties, and soon she was not even able to spell to Keller. She died on March 21, 1960, leaving none of her possessions—which totaled about $130,000—to Keller. Thomson's ashes were placed next to Anne Sullivan's at the National Cathedral.

Keller, who was now eighty-one and becoming frail, had a stroke in October 1961, forcing her to retire from making public appearances. Over the next seven years, she had several other strokes and also suffered from diabetes. The woman who once said, "Life is either a daring adventure or it is nothing," had become an invalid and had to remain either in bed or in a wheelchair.[11]

She was awarded the Presidential Medal of Freedom in 1964 by President Lyndon Johnson and was also elected to the Women's Hall of Fame in 1965, receiving the greatest number of votes along with Eleanor Roosevelt. Keller was too ill to be aware of receiving these honors.

Keller suffered a heart attack in May 1968. She died on June 1 at Arcan Ridge, only weeks before she was to turn eighty-eight. Her ashes were placed alongside Sullivan's and Thomson's at the National Cathedral. In spite of the serious obstacles Keller faced, she had devoted most of her life to helping others.

In the mid-twentieth century, Helen Keller was considered the greatest woman alive in the United States.

"Sometimes I wish these too, too solid limitations would melt; I feel positively bruised with their impacts! Day and night. . . . I am reminded that I cannot see or hear when I know perfectly well that in the eternal sense I do," she once wrote. "I use my limitations as tools, not as my real self. If others are helped through them that is the seventh heaven of happiness for me."[12]

Deaf and blind for nearly all her life, Helen Keller epitomized the courage and determination of the human spirit.

1880—Helen Keller is born in Tuscumbia, Alabama, on June 27.

1882—Develops an illness that leaves her blind and deaf.

1887—Anne Sullivan becomes Helen's teacher; Helen discovers the meaning of language at the water pump.

1888—Visits the Perkins Institution for the Blind in Boston.

1890—Begins voice lessons at the Horace Mann School for the Deaf in Boston.

1894—Attends the Wright-Humason School for the Deaf in New York City.

1896—Father dies; enrolls in the Cambridge School for Young Ladies.

1897—Leaves the Cambridge School and is privately
–1898 tutored.

1900—Enters Radcliffe College.

1903—Publishes autobiography, *The Story of My Life*.

1904—Graduates with honors from Radcliffe College; she and Sullivan buy a farmhouse in Wrentham, Massachusetts.

1905—Anne Sullivan marries John Macy.

1908—Keller writes *The World I Live In*.

1909—Joins the Socialist Party of Massachusetts.

1913—Publishes *Out of the Dark*, a series of essays on socialism.

1914—Macy and Sullivan separate; Polly Thomson becomes part of the household.

1916—Keller becomes romantically involved with Peter Fagan.

1917—Moves to Forest Hills, New York, with Sullivan and Thomson.

1919—Appears in the movie *Deliverance*, based on her life.

1920—Performs on the vaudeville circuit.
−1924

1924—Begins working for the American Foundation for the Blind.

1931—Helps establish uniform Braille code; aids in creating national system of libraries for the blind.

1932—John Macy dies; Keller receives honorary doctor of law degree from University of Glasgow.

1933—Nella Braddy's biography *Anne Sullivan Macy* is published.

1936—Anne Sullivan dies.

1937—Keller travels to Japan on behalf of the blind.

1946—Begins touring for the American Foundation for
−1957   the Overseas Blind.

1948—Travels to Hiroshima, Japan.

1953—*The Unconquered*, a documentary of Keller's life, is released.

1955—Publishes *Teacher*, a biography of Anne Sullivan.

1957—*The Miracle Worker*, a drama based on Helen Keller's childhood, is broadcast live on television.

1960—Polly Thomson dies.

1961—Keller has a stroke.

1964—Awarded the Presidential Medal of Freedom.

1965—Elected to Women's Hall of Fame.

1968—Dies on June 1 after suffering a heart attack.

Chapter Notes

Chapter 1. "No-world"

1. Helen Keller, *The Story of My Life* (New York: Doubleday, Page, 1903), p. 22.

2. Richard Harrity and Ralph G. Martin, *The Three Lives of Helen Keller* (New York: Doubleday & Company, Inc., 1962), p. 31.

3. Taken from a letter written by Anne Sullivan to Mrs. Sophia Hopkins as cited in Dorothy Herrmann, *Helen Keller: A Life* (New York: Alfred A. Knopf, 1998), p. 43.

4. Taken from a letter written by Anne Sullivan to Mrs. Sophia Hopkins as cited in Joseph P. Lash, *Helen and Teacher* (New York: Delacorte Press/Seymour Lawrence, 1980), p. 54.

5. Keller, *The Story of My Life*, p. 9.

6. Ibid., p. 23.

7. Helen Keller, *Teacher* (New York: Doubleday & Company, Inc., 1955), p. 36.

Chapter 2. From Light to Dark

1. Dorothy Herrmann, *Helen Keller: A Life* (New York: Alfred A. Knopf, 1998), p. 6.

2. Joseph P. Lash, *Helen and Teacher* (New York: Delacorte Press/Seymour Lawrence, 1980), p. 45.

3. "Helen Keller, 87, Dies," *The New York Times*, June 2, 1968, p. A76.

4. Lash, p. 43.

5. Helen Keller, *The Story of My Life* (New York: Doubleday, Page, 1903), p. 7.

6. Richard Harrity and Ralph G. Martin, *The Three Lives of Helen Keller* (New York: Doubleday & Company, Inc., 1962), p. 27.

7. Keller, *The Story of My Life*, p. 10.

8. Harrity and Martin, p. 7.

9. Lash, p. 47.

10. Ibid.

11. Keller, *The Story of My Life*, p. 17.

12. Herrmann, p. 23.

Chapter 3. Teacher

1. Helen Keller, *The Story of My Life* (New York: Doubleday, Page, 1903), pp. 18–19.

2. Ibid., p. 19.

3. Dorothy Herrmann, *Helen Keller: A Life* (New York: Alfred A. Knopf, 1998), p. 38.

4. Ibid.

5. Joseph P. Lash, *Helen and Teacher* (New York: Delacorte Press/Seymour Lawrence, 1980), p. 49.

6. Nella Braddy, *Anne Sullivan Macy: The Story Behind Helen Keller* (New York: Doubleday, Doran & Company, Inc., 1933), p. 6.

7. Ibid., p. 39.

8. Ibid., p. 28.

9. Helen Keller, *Teacher* (New York: Doubleday & Company, Inc., 1955), p. 10.

10. Braddy, p. xi.

11. Ibid., p. 63.

12. Lash, p. 30.

13. Braddy, p. 117.

14. Lash, p. 49.

15. Herrmann, p. 40.

16. Keller, *The Story of My Life*, pp. 21–22.

17. "Helen Keller, 87, Dies," *The New York Times*, June 2, 1968, p. A76.

18. Lash, p. 51.

Chapter 4. Beyond Dreams

1. Nella Braddy, *Anne Sullivan Macy: The Story Behind Helen Keller* (New York: Doubleday, Doran & Company, Inc., 1933), p. 121.

2. Joseph P. Lash, *Helen and Teacher* (New York: Delacorte Press/Seymour Lawrence, 1980), p. 51.

3. Helen Keller, *Teacher* (New York: Doubleday & Company, Inc., 1955), p. 49.

4. Braddy, p.121.

5. Ibid., p. 122.

6. Lash, p. 52.

7. Braddy, p. 123.

8. Dorothy Herrmann, *Helen Keller: A Life* (New York: Alfred A. Knopf, 1998), p. 44.

9. Ibid., p. 45.

10. Ibid., p. 208.

11. Naomi S. Baron, *Growing Up with Language: How Children Learn to Talk* (Reading, Mass.: Addison-Wesley Publishing Company, Inc., 1992), p. 53.

12. Helen Keller, *The Story of My Life* (New York: Doubleday, Page, 1903), p. 30.

13. Richard Harrity and Ralph G. Martin, *The Three Lives of Helen Keller* (New York: Doubleday & Company, Inc., 1962), p. 32.

14. Ibid., p. 33.

Chapter 5. Reading, Writing, and 'Rithmetic

1. Richard Harrity and Ralph G. Martin, *The Three Lives of Helen Keller* (New York: Doubleday & Company, Inc., 1962), p. 34.

2. Helen Keller, *The Story of My Life* (New York: Doubleday, Page, 1903), pp. 145–146.

3. Joseph P. Lash, *Helen and Teacher* (New York: Delacorte Press/Seymour Lawrence, 1980), p. 63.

4. Dorothy Herrmann, *Helen Keller: A Life* (New York: Alfred A. Knopf, 1998), p. 355.

5. Ibid., p. 61.

6. Lash, p. 73.

7. American Foundation for the Blind, The Helen Keller Archival Collection, The Helen Keller Papers, Writings by Helen Keller, "Teacher's Sayings," document source not identified, <http://www.afb.org/afb/archives/papers/writingsbyhk/w-teachsay.html> (February 23, 2000).

8. Herrmann, p. 72.

9. Keller, *The Story of My Life*, pp. 162–163.

10. Herrmann, p. 73.

11. Helen Keller, *The World I Live In* (New York: The Century Co., 1904), p. 53.

12. Van Wyck Brooks, *Helen Keller: Sketch for a Portrait* (New York: E. P. Dutton & Co., Inc., 1956), p. 134.

13. Harrity and Martin, p. 37.

14. "Helen Keller, 87, Dies," *The New York Times*, June 2, 1968, p. A76.

15. Harrity and Martin, p. 38.

Chapter 6. Put to the Test

1. Dorothy Herrmann, *Helen Keller: A Life* (New York: Alfred A. Knopf, 1998), p. 80.

2. Ibid., p. 81.

3. Helen Keller, *The Story of My Life* (New York: Doubleday, Page, 1903), p. 64.

4. Ibid., p. 68.

5. Herrmann, p. 84.

6. Keller, *The Story of My Life*, p. 74.

7. Ibid., p. 83.

8. Joseph P. Lash, *Helen and Teacher* (New York: Delacorte Press/Seymour Lawrence, 1980), p. 211.

9. Nella Braddy, *Anne Sullivan Macy: The Story Behind Helen Keller* (New York: Doubleday, Doran & Company, Inc., 1933), p. 180.

10. Lash, p. 214.

11. Keller, *The Story of My Life*, p. 238.

12. Richard Harrity and Ralph G. Martin, *The Three Lives of Helen Keller* (New York: Doubleday & Company, Inc., 1962), p. 57.

13. Herrmann, p. 121.

14. Ibid., p. 122.

15. Keller, *The Story of My Life*, p. 242.

Chapter 7. Higher Education

1. Richard Harrity and Ralph G. Martin, *The Three Lives of Helen Keller* (New York: Doubleday & Company, Inc., 1962), p. 49.

2. Ibid.

3. Ellen M. Plante, *Women at Home in Victorian America* (New York: Facts on File, Inc., 1997), p. xi.

4. "Women's History in America," presented by Women's International Center, <http://www.wic.org/misc/history.htm> (February 23, 2000).

5. Mary Jo Deegan, *Jane Addams and the Men of the Chicago School, 1892–1918* (New Brunswick, N.J.: Transaction Books, 1986), pp. 192–196.

6. Nella Braddy, *Anne Sullivan Macy: The Story Behind Helen Keller* (New York: Doubleday, Doran & Company, Inc., 1933), p. 192.

7. Helen Keller, *Teacher* (New York: Doubleday & Company, Inc., 1955), p. 99.

8. Joseph P. Lash, *Helen and Teacher* (New York: Delacorte Press/Seymour Lawrence, 1980), p. 259.

9. Dorothy Herrmann, *Helen Keller: A Life* (New York: Alfred A. Knopf, 1998), p. 124.

10. American Foundation for the Blind, the Helen Keller Archival Collection, the Helen Keller Papers, Writings by Helen Keller, "An Apology for Going to College," document source not identified, <http://www.afb.org/afb/archives/papers/writingsbyhk/w-apology.htm> (February 23, 2000).

11. Herrmann, p. 126.

12. Keller, *Teacher*, p. 97.

13. Lash, p. 262.

14. Helen Keller, *The Open Door* (New York: Doubleday & Company, Inc., 1957), p. 51.

15. Lash, p. 283.

16. Braddy, p. 199.

17. American Foundation for the Blind, the Helen Keller Archival Collection, the Helen Keller Papers, Writings Concerning Friends and Celebrities, Mark Twain, Letter to Miss Keller from Mark Twain (St. Patrick's Day, 1903), <http://www.afb.org/afb/archives/papers/friends/twain/twain1.html> (February 23, 2000).

18. Helen Keller, *Midstream: My Later Life* (New York: Doubleday, Doran & Company, Inc., 1929), p. 26.

19. Henry Thomas and Dana Lee Thomas, *Fifty Great Modern Lives* (New York: Hanover House, 1956), p. 403.

20. Herrmann, p. 144.

21. Helen Keller, *My Religion* (New York: Doubleday, Page & Company, 1927), p. 38.

22. Helen Keller, *The World I Live In* (New York: Century Co., 1904), p. 7.

23. Ibid., p. 73.

24. American Foundation for the Blind, the Helen Keller Archival Collection, the Helen Keller Papers, Writings by Helen Keller, "My Future As I See It," document source not identified, <http://www.afb.org/archives/papers/writingsbyhk/w-future.html> (February 23, 2000).

Chapter 8. Causes

1. Van Wyck Brooks, *Helen Keller: Sketch for a Portrait* (New York: E. P. Dutton & Co., Inc., 1956), p. 91.

2. Ibid.

3. American Foundation for the Blind, The Helen Keller Archival Collection, The Helen Keller Papers, Writings by Helen Keller, "Braille Magic," document source not identified, <http://www.afb.org/afb/archives/papers/writingsbyhk/w-braille.htm> (February 23, 2000).

4. Joseph P. Lash, *Helen and Teacher* (New York: Delacorte Press/Seymour Lawrence, 1980), p. 365.

5. Nella Braddy, *Anne Sullivan Macy: The Story Behind Helen Keller* (New York: Doubleday, Doran & Company, Inc., 1933), p. 223.

6. Brooks, pp. 88–89.

7. Richard Harrity and Ralph G. Martin, *The Three Lives of Helen Keller* (New York: Doubleday & Company, Inc., 1962), p. 84.

8. Helen Keller, *Teacher* (New York: Doubleday & Company, Inc., 1955), p. 105.

9. Ibid.

10. Dorothy Herrmann, *Helen Keller: A Life* (New York: Alfred A. Knopf, 1998), p. 180.

11. Helen Keller, *Midstream: My Later Life* (New York: Doubleday, Doran & Company, Inc., 1929), p. 93.

12. Lash, p. 377.

13. Ibid.

14. Keller, *My Religion*, p. 198.

15. Herrmann, p. 181.

16. Braddy, p. 243.

17. Herrmann, pp. 187–188.

Chapter 9. Loved Ones

1. Helen Keller, *Teacher* (New York: Doubleday & Company, Inc., 1955), p. 127.

2. Nella Braddy, *Anne Sullivan Macy: The Story Behind Helen Keller* (New York: Doubleday, Doran & Company, Inc., 1933), p. 232.

3. Ibid., p. 239.

4. Ibid., p. 241.

5. Helen Keller, *Midstream: My Later Life* (New York: Doubleday, Doran & Company, Inc., 1929), pp. 172–173.

6. Ibid., p. 178.

7. Ibid., p. 179.

8. "Helen Keller, 87, Dies," *The New York Times*, June 2, 1968, p. A76.

9. Keller, *Midstream*, p. 181.

10. Braddy, p. 248.

11. Ibid., p. 251.

12. Keller, *Midstream*, p. 189.

13. Ibid., p. 210.

14. Van Wyck Brooks, *Helen Keller: Sketch for a Portrait* (New York: E. P. Dutton & Co., Inc., 1956), pp. 80–81.

15. Dorothy Herrmann, *Helen Keller: A Life* (New York: Alfred A. Knopf, 1998), p. 228.

Chapter 10. A Daring Adventure

1. Helen Keller, *My Religion* (New York: Doubleday, Page & Company, 1927), pp. 206–207.

2. Dorothy Herrmann, *Helen Keller: A Life* (New York: Alfred A. Knopf, 1998), p. 255.

3. Helen Keller, *Helen Keller's Journal* (New York: Doubleday, Doran & Company, Inc., 1938), p. 279.

4. Ibid., p. 27–28.

5. Ibid., p. 26–27.

6. Helen Keller, *The Open Door* (New York: Doubleday & Company, Inc., 1957), p. 34.

7. Ibid., p. 54.

8. Van Wyck Brooks, *Helen Keller: Sketch for a Portrait* (New York: E. P. Dutton & Co., Inc., 1956), p. 93.

9. Herrmann, p. 289.

10. Ibid., p. 310.

11. Richard Harrity and Ralph G. Martin, *The Three Lives of Helen Keller* (New York: Doubleday & Company, Inc., 1962), p. 91.

12. Keller, *Helen Keller's Journal*, pp. 302–303.

Further Reading

Bergman, Thomas. *Seeing in Special Ways: Children Living with Blindness.* Milwaukee: Gareth Stevens Children's Books, 1989.

Greenberg, Judith E. *What Is the Sign for Friend?* New York: Franklin Watts, 1985.

Harrity, Richard, and Ralph G. Martin. *The Three Lives of Helen Keller.* New York: Doubleday & Company, Inc., 1962.

Helen Keller in Her Story, BFA/Phoenix Films, 1955. (Starring Helen Keller, this film won the Academy Award for Best Documentary in 1955. It is available on VHS videotape.)

Keller, Helen. *The Story of My Life.* New York: Bantam Doubleday Dell Publishing Group, 1991 (originally published 1903).

Nicholson, Lois P. *Helen Keller: Humanitarian.* New York: Chelsea House Publishers, 1995.

Rankin, Laura. *The Handmade Alphabet.* New York: Dial Books, 1991.

St. George, Judith. *Dear Dr. Bel—Your Friend, Helen Keller.* New York: Beech Tree Books, 1993.

Wepman, Dennis. *Helen Keller.* New York: Chelsea House Publishers, 1987.

Internet Addresses

The American Foundation for the Blind
    <http://www.igc.org/afb/archives/intro.html>

The Perkins School for the Blind
    <http://www.perkins.pvt.k12.ma.us/keller.htm>

Ivy Green, Helen Keller's childhood home
    <http://www.bham.net/keller/home.html>

Louis Braille
    <http://www.rnib.org.uk/wesupply/fctsheet/braille.htm>

Index

Page numbers for photographs are in **boldface** type.